How To
Make Your
Own Will

Visit our How To website at **www.howto.co.uk**

At **www.howto.co.uk** you can engage in conversation with our authors – all of whom have 'been there and done that' in their specialist fields. You can get access to special offers and additional content but most importantly you will be able to engage with, and become a part of, a wide and growing community of people just like yourself.

At **www.howto.co.uk** you'll be able to talk and share tips with people who have similar interests and are facing similar challenges in their lives. People who, just like you, have the desire to change their lives for the better – be it through moving to a new country, starting a new business, growing their own vegetables, or writing a novel.

At **www.howto.co.uk** you'll find the support and encouragement you need to help make your aspirations a reality.

You can go direct to **www.how-to-make-your-own-will.co.uk** which is part of the main How To site.

How To Books strives to present authentic, inspiring, practical information in their books. Now, when you buy a title from **How To Books,** you get even more than just words on a page.

How To
Make Your
Own Will

GORDON BOWLEY LLB

howtobooks

'Let's choose executors and talk of wills.'
Richard II, Act III, Scene II – William Shakespeare.

Published by How To Books Ltd,
Spring Hill House, Spring Hill Road,
Begbroke, Oxford OX5 1RX, United Kingdom
Tel: (01865) 375794. Fax: (01865) 379162.
info@howtobooks.co.uk
www.howtobooks.co.uk

First published 2003
Second edition 2005
Third edition 2007
Fourth edition 2009

ISBN: 978 1 84528 379 7

British Library Cataloguing in Publication Data
A catalogue record for this book is available from the British Library

Produced for How To Books by Deer Park Productions, Tavistock, Devon
Typeset by PDQ Typesetting, Newcastle-under-Lyme, Staffs.
Printed and bound by Bell & Bain Ltd, Glasgow

NOTE: The material contained in this book is set out in good faith for general guidance and no liability
can be accepted for loss or expense incurred as a result of relying in particular circumstances on
statements made in this book and the book is bought and sold on that basis. Laws and regulations are
complex and liable to change, and readers should check the current position with the relevant
authorities before making personal arrangements.

Contents

Preface to the fourth edition

This book was originally written to assist you, whether you wish to prepare your own will or to use a professional to make one for you and the fourth edition has the same aim.

This edition thoroughly updates the third edition to take account of changes in statutory and case law. The changes to inheritance tax and consequences for tax planning brought about by the introduction of the transferable nil-rate inheritance tax band (which is discussed in detail) have been noted and the subject of inheritance is now treated in two chapters, one dealing with the subject in general and the other with reducing liability to the tax.

The book takes a logical step-by step approach to its subject and I hope and believe that it will alert you to the many and broad ranging matters to be considered when you take the important step and 'have your last say'.

I have tried to deal not only with the formal, factual legal requirements and technicalities of making a will and to supply examples of wills which can be easily adapted to meet individual circumstances, but also to incorporate something of what I gained from the experience of making and proving thousands of wills in over 30 years practising as a family solicitor. I have endeavoured to set out the things a solicitor would tell you if you could afford to pay for the time it would take!

Throughout the book I have tried to use as few legal terms as conveniently possible and I have included a glossary to help you to understand those that have been used. The appendix contains examples of various forms referred to in the book, a checklist and specimen wills with notes as to how they may be adapted to individual circumstances and additional clauses for use in less common situations.

The book only deals with the law applicable to England and Wales. Scottish law is different. Moreover, law and practice change frequently and personal circumstances vary considerably. For these reasons, while every effort has been made to ensure that the contents of the book are accurate and up to date, no responsibility is accepted for any loss resulting from acting, or from failure to act, as a result of it and the book is sold and bought on that basis. In particular, changes which might be made to the inheritance tax nil-rate exemption band or tax rates in future Finance Acts, should be borne in mind.

Throughout the book, for simplicity's sake and not for any reasons of gender prejudice, I have assumed that the usual case of the male of the species predeceasing the female will occur and throughout the book, 'he' should be read as 'she' or 'they' where the context and circumstances require.

Crown copyright is acknowledged in respect of all statutory or governmental material quoted in the text.

I hope that you will find the book useful.

Gordon Bowley

Why Should You Make a Will?

IT IS YOUR MONEY AND YOU WANT TO DECIDE WHO SHALL HAVE IT

It is self-evident that after death you can no longer personally manage, control or direct the destination of the assets you have so painstakingly acquired during your life or who is to benefit from what remains of them. Neither is it possible for you personally to have any direct input in the upbringing of your children.

If on death, which comes to us all and sometimes when we least expect it, you leave a valid will, it is possible at least indirectly to influence such matters. If you leave no valid will you are said to die intestate and these matters are decided in the main by the state, which is what few would wish and which sometimes has disastrous consequences. By making a will you will have more control over these and other matters and the flexibility which a will gives will bring peace of mind as to what will happen after your death.

The laws of intestacy do not rank highly on the political agenda and were mostly enacted in 1925. Only occasional and piecemeal revisions have been made since that date. The result is that they are out of date and unsuitable for British society in the twenty-first century in which marriage to a lifetime partner is no longer the norm.

In brief, in the case of death without a valid will, who inherits and deals with the winding up of what you leave (known as your estate) depends upon the size of your estate and what relatives, if any, survive you, and these are both matters of chance. If no relatives within a prescribed degree survive you, the Crown or the Duchies of Lancaster or Cornwall will inherit and wind up your estate, which is something that most people would wish to avoid. Moreover, it is more likely that it will be possible to trace those entitled under your will than to trace perhaps long-lost relatives entitled under the laws of intestacy.

Other problems can arise if you do not leave a valid will:

◆ If the value of your home is high in proportion to the total value of your estate and children or sometimes some other relatives survive you, your spouse or partner might be compelled to sell the family home to pay out the children or other relatives. Similarly if your spouse or partner dies intestate, you might be compelled to sell your home or other assets to pay out the entitlement of in-laws or your partner's relatives who might be people you tolerate rather than like. If you or your spouse or partner die intestate, you cannot rely upon your children, relatives or in-laws, who might have the kindest of intentions towards you, permitting your spouse/partner or yourself (as the case may be) to remain in the family home; their hands may be forced by matrimonial or business problems and they may have no alternative but to compel you to sell property and claim their share of the estate immediately.

◆ If your marriage or civil partnership has broken down but no decree absolute of annulment or divorce has been pronounced at the date of your death, then under the laws of intestacy or under a previous will which you may not have revoked, depending upon the circumstances of your particular case, your surviving civil partner or spouse might inherit the whole or a share of your estate which is totally inconsistent with your wishes.

◆ If you are a person with a cohabitee (domestic partner) with whom you have set up home and you die intestate, your partner has no automatic right to inherit anything from you unless your partnership is a civil partnership and it has been registered under the Civil Partnership Act 2004.

There is no such thing in English law as a 'common law' wife or husband. To inherit, your cohabitee must make a prompt application to a court under the Inheritance (Provision for Family and Dependants) Act 1975, and rely upon the tender mercies of the court. Cohabiting couples who are not legally married or civil partners might receive nothing. Making a will is easier and considerably cheaper than making a claim under the Act.

◆ It is a common mistake to believe that because the family home is in joint names the survivor will automatically be entitled to it on the death of the first to die. This only applies if the joint ownership is ownership as joint tenants and not as tenants in common. If the home is held as tenants in common and one co-owner dies intestate not having made a valid will, his share will pass to his relatives and this will frequently necessitate the sale of the property to pay them out, leaving the survivor homeless.

DO YOU REALLY HAVE NOTHING TO LEAVE BUT YOUR DEBTS?

This may seem to be true at first sight, but not upon further reflection. In a financial sense, you are probably worth more when you are dead than when you are alive; for example, if you are negligently killed in an accident your estate might be entitled to a very large sum by way of damages. If you die within a few years of taking out a life or endowment policy, your estate or the beneficiaries of that policy would certainly receive more than you would have received by surrendering it during your lifetime. Pension schemes may provide substantial death in service provisions either by way of lump sum or pension for those who survive you. Perhaps you own a house and there is a mortgage but the mortgage debt is covered by insurance?

ARE YOU TOO YOUNG AND NOT READY TO DIE?

You might be young, fit and active and not be ready to die but the choice is not yours. Accidents do happen: young people are frequently killed in motor accidents for which they are not responsible and fatal diseases do not only strike down the elderly. In the real world it is not possible to say, 'It will not happen to me' and you will not be given a specific period of notice in advance as to when you must go; you will be leaving life and not employment.

IF YOU HAVE TO GO, YOU SHOULD GO YOUR WAY (OR TRY TO)

The right to determine how to dispose of your body after your death belongs to your executor if you make a will or to the next of kin if you do not make a will. Legally your personal wishes may be ignored, but in practice they are more likely to come to light and be carried out if you record them in a will.

THEY ARE YOUR CHILDREN AND YOU SHOULD DECIDE WHO SHOULD BRING THEM UP

If you die without making proper provision for the appointment of a guardian for any children you have who are under the age of 18, they could be brought up by people you consider to be totally unsuitable, and if you are their only surviving parent, the children could even be taken into care and the family split up. You cannot even rely upon your spouse or partner to care for them; he or she could die in or as the result of the same or a subsequent accident or die of an illness while they are still under age. If you make a will you can choose your children's guardian and who is to bring them up, as long as you do not try to displace a guardian appointed by a court, the children's mother or a father who was married to you at the time of their birth or has been registered in the United Kingdom as the father or a person who has been officially granted guardianship by you. However, a provision in a will can even displace such a mother or father if when you die the children have been living with you under a residence order made by a court.

The ability to appoint a guardian by will is especially important to unmarried mothers because on the death of an unmarried mother, her children's father does not necessarily have the legal powers of a parent or become their guardian.

HASN'T THE GOVERNMENT TAKEN ENOUGH TAX FROM YOU IN YOUR LIFETIME?

If you consider that you have been heavily taxed so far and paid more than your fair share or that you are not rich enough to pay death duties, then you (or your loved ones) may have a very unpleasant surprise. In today's world if you own your house and have a mortgage protection, endowment or life policy, you could well find that you have an inheritance tax problem. Remember that the value of these items and many of the gifts you may have made in the seven years before your death will be added to the value of anything else which you own at your death and that if the total (after deduction of your funeral expenses and any debts you owe) is over the exemption limit (sometimes known as the nil-rate band and which at the present date is £325,000) the excess will be taxed at a full 40%! It is true that what your civil partner or spouse inherits from you is exempt from inheritance tax on your death, but that does not necessarily help in that it will only be added to whatever your spouse or partner owns. Moreover, the exemption does not apply to cohabitees unless they have a registered civil partnership and heterosexual couples and siblings are not permitted to enter into civil partnerships.

By making a will and carefully considering its provisions you may be able to arrange matters so that more of your estate is inherited by those you care for and less by the state; you will be able to make use of the various inheritance tax exemptions and reliefs that exist. Failure to engage in tax planning by making a will can sometimes be considered as leaving a legacy to the state.

SPARING YOUR NEXT OF KIN EXTRA PAIN

Your next of kin might be just too upset to deal with your business affairs when you die or you might not wish him or her to handle your business.

It is only natural that those close to you will be upset when you die and having to repeatedly deal with papers relating to you will only make matters worse.

Your next of kin may not have sufficient business knowledge or
ability to handle your affairs, and if they are complicated you
might wish to entrust them to a professional executor or
knowledgeable and experienced friend. If you have few close
relatives and do not have contact with them, do you really wish a
long-lost cousin to wind up your financial affairs for you after
your death or would you prefer a trusted friend or business
colleague to do it for you? Again on death you might wish to
place your affairs in the hands of your principal beneficiaries or a
combination of several of the above. Making a will gives you the
flexibility in these matters which anyone dying intestate does not
have.

SOME MATTERS ARE REALLY URGENT

Executors derive their powers from the will itself and they come
into effect at the moment the person who made it dies. If a valid
will has not been made, no one has any legal power to act until
someone (who is called an administrator and who is usually the
next of kin) has been appointed to do so by a document called
Letters of Administration issued by the High Court. The
appointment takes some time. Delay can be disastrous if there are
matters requiring urgent attention; for example, you may have
been negligently killed in an accident and have a legal right to
claim for damages which will fail if the claim is not made within
specified time limits, or there might be a family dispute
concerning the funeral arrangements or who is to make them.

WHAT HAPPENS IF YOU DIE WITHOUT A VALID WILL (IN GREATER DETAIL!)

If you die without making a will you are said to die intestate and
your estate will be wound up and inherited according to intestacy

law. Your wishes expressed in any document other than a will will be disregarded.

Who will administer your estate?

Unless your estate is under £5,000 before paying your funeral expenses and debts, or it consists entirely of property held in joint names as joint tenants (as to which see Chapter 3), it will be necessary for someone to be appointed as the administrator of your estate by the Probate Registry at the High Court and given powers to wind it up in accordance with intestacy law. This is done by the Registry granting Letters of Administration of the estate to the appropriate person. You have no right to decide who that person will be. The following people have the right to ask to be appointed and they are entitled in the order set out:

1. Your spouse or civil partner, or if he or she has survived you but dies before obtaining Letters of Administration of your estate, his or her personal representative.
2. Your children or other issue, i.e. children or grandchildren or other descendants.
3. Your father and mother.
4. Your brothers and sisters of the whole blood or their issue.
5. Your brothers and sisters of the half blood or their issue.
6. Your grandparents.
7. Your uncles and aunts of the whole blood or their issue.
8. Your uncles and aunts of the half blood or their issue.
9. The Crown.
10. Your creditors.

Only blood relations and adopted or illegitimate relatives count, not relatives by marriage. Your friends are disregarded. Same sex partners who have not registered their partnership under the Civil

Partnership Act 2004 and different sex partners who are not married to each other have no right to administer their partner's estate no matter how long they have been together.

Who will inherit your estate?
A few general points first.

Again, except for your spouse or civil partner, only blood relationships and adopted or illegitimate relatives count, not relations by marriage. Your friends are disregarded.

The law as to who will inherit your estate if you die intestate divides your relatives into groups or classes according to their relationship to you, e.g. children, siblings, grandparents, etc. All members of a given class inherit in equal shares. If a member of a class has died before you and leaves issue who survive you, the issue inherit equally between them the share which their predeceasing parent would have inherited had he survived you. There is a specific order in which the various classes inherit and if all members of a given class have died before you without leaving issue who survive you, the next class inherits. The words 'child' and 'children' are used to mean your immediate descendants (as opposed to grandchildren) and the word 'issue' is used to mean all your descendants. If those entitled to inherit are under the age of 18, the inheritance is held in trust for them until they either reach the age of 18 or enter into a registered civil partnership or marry under that age. If your civil partner or spouse does not survive you by 28 days your estate is distributed as if he or she had not survived you. Net estate means the estate after deducting all debts, liabilities, inheritance tax and funeral and testamentary expenses.

To decide who will be entitled to inherit your estate when you die it will be necessary to look for the first class and if there is no member of that class who survives you or predeceases you leaving issue who survive you, to move on to the next class.

The first person to have a claim on your estate will be your civil partner or surviving spouse and the amount to which he or she will be entitled will depend upon the size of the net estate and whether or not there are any surviving issue or certain other close relatives. If your spouse or registered civil partner survives, but for a period of less than 28 days beginning on the day on which you die, he or she is considered not to have survived you.

If you leave a surviving spouse or civil partner but no issue and no parent, brother or sister of the whole blood or issue of a brother or sister of the whole blood, your spouse or civil partner will inherit the entire estate.

If you leave a surviving spouse or civil partner and issue or any of the specified relatives, your spouse or civil partner will be entitled to your personal chattels, i.e. moveable items such as sporting trophies or motor car, but personal chattels does not include items used in any business, e.g. a delivery van.

Your spouse or civil partner is also entitled to be paid a fixed sum of money known as a statutory legacy out of your estate and interest on the statutory legacy at the rate of 2% from the date of death until the administrator of your estate pays it to her.

If you are survived by issue your spouse's or partner's statutory legacy is £250,000. If you leave no surviving issue but leave a surviving parent, or a brother or sister of the whole blood or issue of a brother or sister of the whole blood who has died before you, the legacy is £450,000.

Your surviving spouse or civil partner will also be entitled to one half of what is known as 'the residuary estate', i.e. what remains of the net estate after deducting the personal chattels and the statutory legacy. If you also leave surviving issue, your civil partner or spouse will be entitled to the share of the residuary estate only during her lifetime, but if you leave no surviving issue, then your spouse or civil partner is entitled to the share for her use and benefit absolutely. When your spouse or partner is only entitled to the half share of the residuary estate for the remainder of her life, then because it has to be left for those who are entitled to inherit it after her death, she can only spend the income that share produces and cannot spend the capital sum represented by the share. Where your spouse or civil partner is entitled to the share for her own use and benefit absolutely she can, of course, dispose of both the capital and income as she wishes.

Your surviving spouse or civil partner is entitled to require your personal representative to use the remaining residuary estate to purchase her interest for life in the one half share of your residuary estate from her. If your home is freehold or leasehold with at least two years of the lease to run at the date of your death, your spouse or civil partner can also insist upon using her share of the residuary estate to buy the home, paying any difference in value in cash. To exercise either of these two rights your spouse or partner must give notice of her intention to do so to your personal representatives within a year of the issue of the grant of Letters of Administration of your estate. If your spouse or civil partner is your sole personal representative the notice should be given to The Senior Registrar of The Family Division of The High Court of Justice. In cases where the home

- is part of a building or agricultural estate contained in the residuary estate or
- is used in part or entirely as a hotel or lodging house or
- in part for other than domestic purposes

the right cannot be exercised unless a court is satisfied that it is not likely to diminish the value of the other assets in the residuary estate or make them more difficult to dispose of.

If you leave a surviving spouse or civil partner and issue, the issue will inherit one half of the residuary estate on your death and the other one half of the residuary estate after the death of your surviving spouse or partner.

If you leave a surviving spouse or civil partner but no issue, she will inherit one half of the residuary estate for her own use and benefit absolutely and the other one half share of the residuary estate is inherited by your parent if one survives you and if both survive you then by them in equal shares, or if no parent has survived, by your brothers or sisters of the whole blood and issue of deceased brothers and sisters of the whole blood, the issue of your deceased brothers or sisters inheriting equally between them the share which their deceased parent would have taken had he survived you.

If you leave no surviving spouse or civil partner but leave issue the issue inherit the net estate.

If you leave no surviving spouse or civil partner and leave no issue but leave a parent or parents who survive you, the net estate is inherited by your parent, and if both survive you, then by them equally.

If you leave no spouse, civil partner, issue or parent, the net estate is inherited by the following classes of people who are living at your death and in the following order so that if there is no one in a class living at the death the subsequent class inherit, namely your brothers and sisters of the whole blood, or if none, your brothers and sisters of the half blood, or if none, your grandparents, or if none, your uncles and aunts of the whole blood, or if none, your uncles and aunts of the half blood.

If you leave none of the above your estate goes to the Crown, the Duchy of Cornwall or the Duchy of Lancaster.

A person is considered to be your spouse for the purposes of the laws of intestacy when once you have married them until a decree absolute (not a decree nisi) of divorce or nullity or a judicial separation (other than in the magistrates court) has been made in respect of the marriage and to be your civil partner from when the partnership is registered until it is dissolved.

Your children will only have a right to their inheritance under the above provisions when they attain the age of 18 or enter into a registered civil partnership or marry under that age, whichever happens first, but there are provisions for the administrator of the estate to use up to one half of a child's potential share for the child's benefit before the relevant event occurs.

'Children' does not include stepchildren under the law as to inheritance on intestacy. Adopted children inherit on intestacy from their adoptive parents but not from their natural parents.

For the purpose of inheritance, if you are unmarried and you conceive a child artificially i.e. by fertilisation by a donor, as the result of treatment provided for you and the man together, the donor of the sperm is considered to be the father of the child; if you are married and not judicially separated and you conceive a child artificially, your husband is considered to be the father of the child, unless it is proved that he did not consent to the fertilisation. These rules do not apply to inheritance of a title or land which devolves with the title.

What will happen to your business?
Under the general law your executors, or your administrators if you do not make a will and die intestate, have power to carry on the business without restrictions on that power, only for the purpose of winding it up and that should be done within one year. To do so might be impractical or economically disadvantageous. If they take longer than a year your personal representatives can be held liable in law for any debts and losses incurred. If you run or are likely to run a business and you make a will you can provide in the will that your executors shall have power to carry on the business either alone or in partnership for any purpose or period and provide that they shall be entitled to be indemnified out of the business for any debts or liabilities reasonably incurred in so doing.

Have I convinced you that you need a will?

Then do not delay. Let us make one now before it is too late.

Can You Make a Will and How to Do It

CAN YOU MAKE A WILL?

Do you have the required understanding?

To be entitled to make a will (as opposed to having a court make a will for you and deciding what that will shall be) you must have the required degree of understanding (valid testamentary capacity). Even after the coming into force of the Mental Capacity Act 2005 (which defined mental capacity for most legal purposes) and the code of practice made under the authority of the Act (which gives a judge discretion to use the definition contained in the Act to decide the question of capacity to make a will), it is still the usual practice for the mental capacity to make a will to be decided upon Common Law principles. Under the Common Law, to have testamentary capacity, in addition to being over the age of 18 (unless you are a seaman at sea or you are in the armed forces and on active military service), you must be able to

* understand roughly what making a will means, i.e. the nature of the transaction you are entering into, that it only takes effect on death and can be changed before you die;

* have a rough idea of what you have to leave;

* be aware of the moral claims of those you are benefiting in the will and those you have a moral obligation to benefit (although

you are not under a legal obligation to leave them anything); and

◆ understand in broad terms the effect of the will without your decisions being affected by mental disorder.

A distinction is drawn between being capable of understanding and actually understanding and in the event of a dispute as to your testamentary capacity proof that you actually understood, as opposed to the fact that you were capable of understanding, is not required.

You are assumed to have testamentary capacity unless it is proved that you lack capacity and unless it is proved that you lack capacity the provisions of your will may be as unwise, imprudent, capricious, spiteful and eccentric as you wish.

You may have testamentary capacity and be able to make a valid will even though you are of unsound mind and suffering from delusions in some respects, as long as that insanity does not affect the above points. For example, you may have good testamentary capacity even though you are convinced that the world is a cube.

The fact that you are unable for physical or educational reasons to read or write or that you can only sign your name by making your mark, does not prevent you from making your will; these difficulties can be dealt with in the wording of the will as we shall see later.

If you have the necessary mental capacity and are a member of the armed forces engaged in actual military service or are a seaman at sea, then notwithstanding the fact that you may be under the age of 18, you can make an informal will which will not be revoked by merely leaving the service or in the case of a seaman, returning to land.

Your will will not become invalid if you become totally insane or otherwise lose your testamentary capacity after making it, as long as you had testamentary capacity at the time you made it. Even if you are normally mentally incapable, you are legally able to make a valid will in any lucid period.

If you ask someone else, for example a solicitor, to prepare a will for you, the will will be valid if you had testamentary capacity at the time you gave the instructions for the preparation of the will, even if it is doubtful whether you had testamentary capacity at the time you signed the will, provided that at the time you signed the will you understood that it put into effect the instructions which you had given for the will.

Proving you have the required understanding
If your will is rational on the face of it at the relevant time and appears to have been properly completed, there will be a rebuttable presumption that it is valid and that you had full testamentary capacity when you made it. The burden of proving that this was not so will be upon those who seek to challenge the will. However if there is credible evidence that you did not have the required testamentary capacity when you made the will, the burden of proving that you did have the required mental capacity will then pass to your executors. If your capacity is likely to be challenged it might be sensible to ask your doctor to examine you and to witness the will.

Making a will if you do not have the required understanding

If you are over the age of 18 and do not have testamentary capacity, The Court of Protection can be requested to authorise the making of a will for you under powers given to it by The Mental Capacity Act 2005. Such a will is known as a statutory will and will be made to benefit those whom *you* personally might be expected to benefit by your will if you had competent legal advice and testamentary capacity and not those who a hypothetical person in your position might be expected to benefit. As Vice-Chancellor Megarry said 'It is the actual patient who has to be considered who may have had strong antipathies or deep affections for particular persons or causes, and not a hypothetical patient. The court must take the patient as he or she was before losing testamentary capacity, with allowance being made for the passage of years.' The court will not usually make a will solely for tax planning purposes.

Application for authority to sign the statutory will on your behalf is usually made to the court by an attorney appointed by you by a Lasting Power of Attorney or a deputy appointed by the court and supporting evidence should include evidence of your mental capacity, a copy of any existing will, a draft of the proposed new will, confirmation that the proposed executors are willing to act, evidence of your life expectancy, details of your assets, income and expenditure, similar details in respect of the proposed beneficiaries and a statement of the tax implications of what is proposed.

Although an application for the making of a statutory will is expensive and the cost is usually ordered to be paid out of your assets unless the application is considered to have been made unreasonably (in which case the applicant might be ordered to bear the cost), the expense might be justified by the reasons for making a will which are set out in Chapter 1, especially if there have been major changes in your financial or other circumstances since you lost your capacity or made your previous will.

The power of the court to make a will includes the power to revoke an existing will.

COMPLYING WITH THE FORMALITIES

Members of the armed forces engaged in actual military service and seamen at sea can make informal wills without observing any formalities whatsoever: their wills can be made irrespective of their age, do not have to be witnessed and need not be made in writing. Unless you fall within those categories there are some formalities which must be observed if your will is to be valid and legally enforceable.

The remainder of this chapter applies to any will that you make in England or Wales. The formalities for making wills while you are abroad or for making what are known as 'international wills' are dealt with in Chapter 9.

The formalities, which are legally required and are essential in respect of wills which you make in England or Wales, are as follows.

YOUR WILL MUST BE MADE IN WRITING

Your will can be in any form of writing, handwritten, typed or printed, and in any language, but it *must be in writing* and any other expression of your wishes will not be effective. Oral expressions of your wishes and wills recorded on sound-tapes or videotapes are therefore not valid wills.

Your will should be written *legibly* because what cannot be read cannot be enforced. You do not necessarily have to write out the will yourself but if a beneficiary writes out the will by hand for you, suspicions might arise as to whether or not you knew of and approved of the contents of the will when you signed it and it could be challenged.

Your will can be written *on any material*, on paper, parchment, linen or carved in stone if you wish. Certain stationers sell 'will forms' upon which the basic parts of a will are pre-printed and on which you only have to fill in the blanks, but for some reason or another people always seem to have difficulty in filling them in correctly. In over 35 years practising as a solicitor I cannot recollect seeing more than a dozen will forms which had been correctly completed. As in all other matters relating to wills, when considering the material upon which your will is to be written, it is better to keep it simple and use a blank sheet of good quality paper because with good luck and a healthy lifestyle it will be many years before your will will be required to be proved! If you use ink, use permanent ink. Although to do so would not make your will invalid, for reasons of security do not use pencil or a writing media which can be easily erased. Not everyone is honest in financial matters!

YOUR WILL MUST BE SIGNED BY YOU OR BY SOMEONE IN YOUR PRESENCE AND AT YOUR REQUEST

The signature need not be your full name or indeed your name at all as long as a court will be satisfied that the mark which is made was intended as your signature and that it was intended to authenticate the document as your will. I always told clients to sign their will in the same way as they would sign their cheques on the basis that if the mark intended as a signature can extract money from their bank account it can do anything! An inked thumbprint has been held by a court to be a sufficient signature, as has the testator's initials impressed by his seal, but the courts have not yet accepted electronic signatures and it is best to keep it simple and avoid courts rather than tempt fate by using such esoteric forms of authentication.

In whatever way your will is signed, it must either be done by you personally or by someone for you, at your direction and in your presence. To avoid problems, you should always sign your will personally or at least make a mark as your signature if you possibly can. If you are physically unable to sign or make your mark, e.g. because of paralysis or because you are blind, you can ask someone to sign the will for you as your will but they must do so in your presence and in the presence of the required witnesses.

YOUR SIGNATURE ON THE WILL MUST BE MADE OR ACKNOWLEDGED BY YOU IN THE PRESENCE OF TWO OR MORE WITNESSES WHO MUST BE PRESENT AT THE SAME TIME

If all the witnesses to your will are not with you when the will is signed, you must confirm to them that the signature is yours and all the witnesses must be there when you do so. It is not sufficient for you to confirm it to each witness on separate occasions or for you to sign in the presence of one or more witnesses when the others are not there and subsequently to confirm the signature to the absent witness or witnesses.

Although the Wills Act 1837 refers to two or more wit[...] only necessary and usual to have two witnesses to your signature, but they must be of age and mentally capable.

EACH WITNESS MUST SIGN THE WILL AND EITHER SIGN OR ACKNOWLEDGE HIS SIGNATURE IN YOUR PRESENCE

You must be present when the witness signs or acknowledges his signature, but there is no necessity for each witness to be present when the other witness signs.

IT MUST BE APPARENT THAT YOU INTEND TO GIVE EFFECT TO THE WILL BY SIGNING IT

In practice your signature and those of the witnesses should appear at the end of the will to show that they are intended to give effect to all that goes before the signatures as your will. If words appear in the will after the signatures there can be problems in that the Probate Registry will insist on the witnesses swearing an affidavit or making an affirmation to confirm that the words were in your will when it was signed and not added later by you or by anyone else and the witnesses might not then be alive, traceable or able to recollect. If the words were added later, of course, they would be ineffective, invalid and would not be admitted to probate.

If there are more pages than one it is as well for yourself and the witnesses to also sign at the bottom of each page so that nothing can be added later to the page and for the pages to be numbered so that no further pages can be inserted.

It is usual to indicate in the wording of the will that the document is signed as your last will. See the specimen wills in the appendix.

A FEW GENERAL WORDS ON THE SUBJECT OF SIGNING THE WILL AND WITNESSES

The witnesses are witnessing your signature. It follows therefore that you must sign first or there will be nothing for them to witness. The witnesses must be in a position to see you sign, not blind and their view must not be obscured. The witnesses need not know the contents of the will or even that it is a will, because it is your signature that they are witnessing and not the document, but it is necessary that they should not merely see the document but also intend to verify, i.e. attest, the signature that is being witnessed.

When are you and the witness in each other's presence? When each can see what the other is doing, even if you are not in the same room.

All the above requirements as to the witnessing of wills might seem complicated but if you ensure that

- yourself and two adult witnesses are all present in the same room before any signing begins

- the witnesses are not blind

- the witnesses are not beneficiaries or the executors of the will or the spouse or civil partner of any beneficiary or executor (if they are the will will be valid but the beneficiary will lose the bequest and the executor possibly his right to expenses unless specifically authorised to charge them or the will is an informal military one or a seaman's will made at sea)

- the witnesses are likely to be traceable if required when you die

- you sign first followed by each witness

- each witness signs with his usual signature and follows it by his printed name and his address and occupation or status (married woman, widow, etc.) if a woman and

- no one leaves the room before the signing is complete

there should be no problem.

CONVENTIONS

There are other traditional practices which, while they are not legal requirements and will not invalidate your will if they are not followed, are conventions used in the layout of wills and which will give your will a classy, professional appearance. These are as follows:

1. The will should be laid out in paragraphs numbered in sequence after a first paragraph which confirms the nature of the document (will or codicil) and states your name, address and occupation or, if you are a woman without an occupation, your status (married woman, widow etc.). The first words of each paragraph should be in block capitals and underlined.

2. The order of the paragraphs should be

   a) a clause beginning I REVOKE to revoke all previous testamentary dispositions if that is your intention;

   b) a clause beginning I APPOINT which deals with the appointment of executors and trustees;

   c) a clause beginning I GIVE which sets out any legacies of money which you might wish to make;

   d) a clause beginning I BEQUEATH which sets out any gifts of specific articles which you wish to make;

   e) a clause beginning I BEQUEATH which sets out any gifts of leasehold property;

f) a clause beginning I DEVISE which sets out any gifts of freehold land or buildings;

g) a clause beginning I GIVE DEVISE BEQUEATH AND APPOINT which deals with any remaining property you may have to dispose of;

h) separate clauses or sub-clauses giving your executors additional powers or excluding powers which the law gives them by default;

i) a clause beginning I EXPRESS the wish, which sets out your wishes in relation to your funeral and the disposal of your body after your death;

j) a clause beginning IN WITNESS explaining that you have signed your will and stating the date on which it is signed unless the date has been stated in the introductory paragraph; and finally

k) a clause called an attestation clause that explains the circumstances in which the will was signed and witnessed beginning SIGNED. If you are unable to read, this clause should explain that the will had been read over to you before you signed it and the two witnesses then signed it in your presence. In these circumstances it should also state that you understood and approved the will. If you are unable to sign the will, the clause should explain that it is signed by a named person for you, at your request and in the joint presence of yourself and two witnesses, who then signed the will in your presence and the presence of the person who signed for you. Suitable forms of attestation clause can be found in the appendix to this book.

3. All names should be set out in full, in capitals and underlined.

4. Sums of money should be stated in words in underlined block capitals followed by the sum in brackets in figures.

Reference to the specimen wills in the appendix to this book will make the above points clearer.

TAKING PRECAUTIONS AGAINST FRAUD

As a precaution against the possibility of subsequent tampering with the will and fraud:

1. The date of the will should be expressed in words rather than figures (words are more difficult to alter than figures) and any sums of money should be expressed in words followed by the sum in brackets expressed in figures.

2. Each page of the will should be numbered and signed by you and by the witnesses as close to the last line on the page as possible to prevent anything being inserted.

3. Try to avoid making any alterations, interlineations or obliterations, but if they are unavoidable, you and the witnesses should each write his or her respective initials as close as possible to them to authenticate them.

4. The gaps at the end of each line and paragraph should be ruled through.

5. The same pen should be used by you and by the witnesses when signing to indicate that all signed at the same time.

6. If you are blind or otherwise unable to read, have someone other than the person who prepared the will read it over to you before it is signed.

7. Consider depositing your completed will with the Probate Registry for safe custody as explained in detail in Chapter 11, pages 183–4.

Finally never, never attach, pin or fasten anything to the will, even with a paperclip.

What You Can Leave By Your Will

GENERAL PRINCIPLES

Whether you can or cannot leave moveable property (i.e. anything other than land, which includes non-portable buildings on land) by your will is decided by the law of the state in which you are domiciled, i.e. the state which is considered to be your permanent home at the date of your death. Whether you can or cannot leave immoveable property by your will is decided by the law of the state in which the land is situated.

You cannot be without a domicile and you cannot have more than one domicile at any given time. At birth you have the same domicile as your mother if you are illegitimate or your father is dead, otherwise the domicile of your father. This is known as your domicile of origin.

You can exchange your domicile of origin for what is known as a domicile of choice by abandoning your ties with the state in which you have your domicile of origin and moving to live in another state *with the intention of making it your permanent home or residing there indefinitely.* Your domicile of choice can be abandoned by ceasing to reside in and abandoning your ties to the relevant state *and* ceasing to intend to reside there permanently or indefinitely. If you abandon a domicile of choice without acquiring a new domicile of choice you re-acquire your domicile of origin. A new domicile of choice can be acquired as frequently as you wish, but you can only have one domicile at any given time.

Those who are mentally incapable or under the age of 16 have the domicile of the person upon whom they are dependent and their domicile will follow any change in that person's domicile. This is known as a domicile of dependency. A woman who married before 1 January 1974 acquired her husband's domicile by virtue of the marriage, but after that date she can change it and her domicile is no longer dependent upon her husband.

There are exceptions to the above rules for inheritance tax purposes, in that for those purposes,

- you are deemed to retain your domicile in the relevant part of the United Kingdom for three years after leaving it and

- you are deemed to be domiciled here if you have been resident here for any part of 17 or more of the 20 preceding *tax* years.

I use the word 'state' in connection with domicile rather than 'country' because domicile is defined not by national boundaries but by places which have their own independent system of law.

If your domicile is England and Wales you can dispose by will of anything in England and Wales and any moveable property which you have abroad and you can dispose of it to whom you wish and to the exclusion of your family unless

- you have restricted yourself by contract, e.g. by entering into an agreement to create and not revoke mutual wills; or

- it is something which does not pass to your personal representative on your death, e.g. jointly owned property held as joint tenants; or

♦ it is a contract in which your personality is an essential element, e.g. a contract to paint a portrait or to write a book; or

♦ it is property you do not own (e.g. assurance policies taken out by you on trust for another) and over which you have not been given a power of appointment; or

♦ the property has been 'nominated' and the nomination has not been revoked; or

♦ it is property the disposal of which is restricted by its nature, e.g. some rights in immoveable property such as a personal licence or permission to use or cross the land of another, or shares in some small companies; or

♦ it is your body; or

♦ statute law restricts your right to dispose of it in the way you wish.

Some of these matters are easy to understand but I will deal with the others in more detail.

MUTUAL WILLS

Mutual wills must not be confused with so called 'mirror wills'.

Mirror wills are merely wills each of which precisely reflects or mirrors the terms of the other and are frequently entered into by husband and wife. They are nothing more than wills with reciprocal terms. Mutual wills are wills made by one testator under a legally binding contract with another testator to make the wills and not revoke them without the other's consent. The contract need not be a written one unless the will disposes of an interest in land.

To be a legally binding contract the agreement must

- be intended to create a legally binding relationship;

- have an element of bargain, i.e. of a mutual exchange of promises.

The fact that two people make their wills together at the same time and in identical terms does not by itself make them mutual wills. To be mutual wills there must also be further evidence of a legal contract to make the bequest and not revoke it without the beneficiary's consent. Extrinsic evidence, i.e. evidence which is not apparent from the wills themselves (e.g. a separate mutual wills agreement or letters exchanged between the parties concerned), can be used to show that what on the face of it appear to be mirror wills were in fact mutual wills. A form of mutual will agreement is included in the appendix to this book.

Makers of mutual wills need not necessarily confer benefits upon each other by their wills, provided that the agreement and the above elements of a contract are present. For example, A and B might agree that A will give up A's house and go to live with and act as a carer for B for the remainder of their joint lives, if B will leave B's house to A by will and not revoke the gift and further that A will leave the house to B's children in A's will. Another example of mutual wills would be if two partners in a business mutually agree to leave their share in the business each to the other by their wills and not to revoke the bequests.

In English law a will cannot be made irrevocable, but if one party to an agreement for mutual wills breaks the agreement, the other party is released from it and is free to make alternative provisions in that other party's will.

If one party to a mutual wills agreement dies having carried out his part of the bargain and the other party makes a new will in breach of the agreement, then upon the death of the party who has broken the agreement a court would ensure that the effect of the agreement is achieved either by granting damages in favour of the aggrieved party's estate against the other estate or imposing a trust upon his estate to achieve justice for the aggrieved party's estate. On the death of the first to die the trust immediately binds the assets then the subject of the mutual will agreement and not merely what is left of them when the survivor dies. To put it another way, the property bound by the mutual will agreement is all the property the subject of the agreement which the survivor inherits and not merely what is left of it when he dies. The survivor is not free to dispose of it or reduce its value during his lifetime and to consider that the agreement only applies to what is left when he has had his way with it!

Exactly what assets are the subject of the mutual will agreement is a question to be decided by construing the agreement.

Mutual wills are useful if it is considered that it is likely that the survivor will be pressurised and bullied to change his will after the first death.

If you are in a second marriage or civil partnership, you might wish to consider making mutual wills with a view to ensuring that your second spouse or partner is provided for after your death but your estate is inherited on your spouse's or partner's death by the children of your first relationship and not your second spouse's or second partner's children. In these circumstances you should consider whether the desired result might be better achieved by non-mutual wills in which each spouse or partner leaves a life interest to the other, the estate thereafter to be inherited by the children of the first relationship.

Although the law will not usually enforce a promise made in your lifetime to make a gift by your will and your executor cannot legally carry it out unless it is contained in a valid will or codicil or in a binding contract to make mutual wills, the law will very exceptionally enforce such a promise if the potential beneficiary reasonably relies upon it to his detriment in such circumstances that the promise would bind you in all conscience to do no other than to carry out your promise. The essential factors which must be present are a clear promise intended to be relied upon and which might reasonably be expected to be relied upon by the person to whom it was made, reliance upon it, detriment and extremely seriously unconscionable conduct. In these extreme circumstances the judge also has a discretion to order a financial payment of a lower value instead of fully compensating the claimant's loss.

JOINTLY OWNED PROPERTY, i.e. PROPERTY NOT IN YOUR SOLE NAME

There are two ways of owning property jointly in English law, namely as joint tenants or as tenants in common. The use of the word 'tenants' has nothing to do with tenants in the sense of landlord and tenant; it is merely the same word used as a technical term to signify a different concept.

If people own property as joint tenants, the law provides that on the death of one owner, that person's share is inherited by the surviving joint owner or owners by the very act of surviving, regardless of the terms of the deceased's will or the next of kin, but a share of property which is owned as tenants in common is inherited on death as provided for in the deceased's will, if there is one, or if none, then by the next of kin in accordance with the intestacy laws.

How do you know whether jointly owned property was held as joint tenants or tenants in common? Usually bank accounts, building society accounts and stocks and shares in joint names are held as joint tenants, but if there is any evidence to show that the joint owners owned separate shares of the property as opposed to each joint owner owning the entirety, the joint ownership is a case of tenancies in common. The regular sharing by the joint owners of the dividends from jointly owned shares in a company in the same unequal proportions might be an example of such evidence. Joint tenants always own the asset equally and words or actions indicating that the joint owners own unequally always means that the assets are held as tenants in common. Partnerships almost invariably own property as tenants in common. When husbands and wives or registered civil partners own property jointly they usually, but not necessarily, do so as joint tenants and not tenants in common.

Because you cannot leave your entitlement in property which you co-own as a joint tenant by will, if you wish to do so you must first sever the joint tenancy to create a tenancy in common and then leave your share by your will. A form of document to sever a joint tenancy and create a tenancy in common is included in the appendix of forms to this book and when completed must be given to the other joint tenant(s) to be effective. It is a wise precaution to arrange for the other co-owner(s) to sign a receipt to confirm that they have received the document and to place the receipted copy of the document with the title documents. If the property has a title which is registered at HM Land Registry, the receipted copy should be sent to the Land Registry at the District Land Registry (which you will find noted on your official copy of the Land Registry title information document) for noting in the Registry's records. When communicating with the Land Registry you should quote the Land Registry Title Number which appears in the copy of the Land Registry title information document.

It is possible for joint tenants to sever the joint tenancy and create a tenancy in common by other conduct showing a shared intention to do so, but such a severance is much more difficult to prove and the burden of proving that severance has taken place is upon the person alleging it.

Whether the jointly owned property is held as joint tenants or as tenants in common your entitlement in the property is included in the value of your estate for the purpose of calculating inheritance tax.

BUSINESS PARTNERSHIPS

If you are a partner in a business you should refer to the written

partnership agreement if one exists. Partnership agreements
frequently provide that on the death of a partner, the surviving
partners shall have a right to buy his share, or less frequently, that
the deceased partner's share shall accrue to the surviving partners
without payment. Such provisions will obviously restrict your right
to leave your share in the partnership to whom you wish.

If there is no written partnership agreement, then on your death
the partnership will cease and the business should be wound up.
Your estate will be entitled to your share of the partnership assets
or the proceeds that their sale produces and they can be left by
your will.

PROPERTY YOU DO NOT OWN

Insurance policies taken out or held on trust for another

It is possible when taking out an insurance policy to stipulate that
the policy is taken out on trust for, i.e. for the benefit of, another
person or people. It is similarly possible to make a written
declaration in respect of an existing policy that the policy shall be
held on trust for others. The main advantages of following these
procedures are that on death or maturity the proceeds of the
policy do not form part of your estate and consequently they are:

◆ immediately payable to the trustees upon production of proof
  of death without waiting for a grant of probate of your will or
  letters of administration of your estate being issued by the
  Probate Registry;

◆ not subject to inheritance tax.

Because the policy is held on trust and is not beneficially owned by you, it is not yours to leave and cannot be included in your will.

Other property you do not own over which you have a power of appointment

Sometimes a deed or another person's will or a trust, while it does not give you property, will give you a right (i.e. power) to decide who shall have the property. This is called a *power of appointment.* The document which gives you the power usually states whether you can use the power by deed in your lifetime or by will or by deed or will.

Other property you do not own over which you have no power of appointment

Although it might seem to be stating the obvious, you should always check that you do in fact own property you purport to give away in your will. It is easy to believe that you own articles which you have on hire purchase which in fact you only hire and are actually owned by the finance company, or consider that you own an assurance policy which you took out on trust for your wife or children. Similarly you may look upon the holiday cottage you inherited from your grandmother as your own and after many years forget that she only left it to you for the duration of your life and that her will provided that thereafter it was to go to another grandson. If you try to leave it by your will to your daughter and you leave a legacy to the grandson, the result will be something that you almost certainly do not expect. There is a rule in English law known as the doctrine of election to the effect that a person who accepts a benefit conferred by a document must also accept every other provision of that document and give up any other right he possesses which is inconsistent with the document. Thus if a testator who does not own something purports to give it away by his will and also gives a bequest to the true owner of the asset, the true owner must either refuse his bequest or give up his own property or its value in compensation to the other beneficiary. Therefore, in the above example, the grandson will have to decide whether he will refuse the legacy or alternatively accept it and give up the cottage (or the value of the cottage) to your daughter.

NOMINATED PROPERTY

There have been various Acts of Parliament which authorised those who deposited money with certain organisations, e.g. National Savings and Friendly Societies, to 'nominate' people to receive the deposits on the depositor's death. Such nominations are not overridden by the provisions of a will, and although it is no longer possible to make new nominations, any deposits which you have made and nominated cannot be left in your will unless the nomination is revoked by signing the organisation's specified form or by your subsequent marriage, or are frustrated by the death of the nominee before your death.

PROPERTY WHICH BY ITS NATURE HAS RESTRICTED ALIENABILITY

Some existing rights in relation to land

Some existing rights for the benefit of land can only be left by will to a beneficiary to whom the land is left; for example, a right of way which you own cannot be left separately from the land or building to which it relates (unless you are giving the right by will or codicil to the owner of the land over which it exists so that it thereby ceases to exist). However, you can give a new right of way over your land by your will to a neighbour for use with his neighbouring land.

Shares in some limited companies

Some family companies and some private companies state in their Articles of Association (the regulations which govern the running of the company) that you cannot transfer shares in the company (sometimes except to specified members of your family), even as the result of a gift in a will, without first offering them to the other shareholders in the company. If you own shares in a small or family company you should check the position first with the company secretary before deciding to whom you will leave them in your will.

Your body

The general rule is that it is not possible to 'own' a dead body. It follows therefore that you cannot leave your body by your will although the courts have decided in a criminal case that if body parts have changed their nature as the result of skill, such as being dissected or preserved for the purpose of exhibition or teaching, they can be property and the subject of theft.

Although you cannot leave your body by will, if you express a wish at any time in writing or during your last illness orally in the presence of two witnesses to the effect that your body, or any part of it, shall be used for therapeutic purposes or for the purpose of medical education, research or anatomical examination, then the person having lawful possession of it (unless he has such possession only for the purpose of its interment or cremation) may authorise such use. Similarly any such person may authorise such use of any part of your body if, after making all reasonable practical enquiries, he has no reason to believe that you or your surviving spouse or relatives would object.

The coroner's prior approval is required for such use if an inquest or coroner's post-mortem may be required.

Your executors have a right and a duty to claim your body and arrange for its disposal.

More detailed information as to the disposal of your body is given in the next chapter.

STATUTORY RESTRICTIONS ON YOUR RIGHT TO LEAVE YOUR ASSETS TO WHOM YOU CHOOSE

Statutory tenancies

Certain old tenancies of private houses and housing association properties and certain tenancies of local authority houses can pass to particular members of your family on your death, but the position is very complicated and professional advice should be sought.

However, it is interesting to note that in 2002, in the case of *Ghaidan v Mendoza*, the court decided that a provision of the Rent Act 1997 which permitted a bequest of a statutory tenancy to a person living with a tenant 'as his or her husband or wife' must be construed to mean 'as if they were his or her husband or wife' and include same-sex couples to avoid contravening the provisions of the European Convention for the Protection of Human Rights and Fundamental Freedoms 1950 as set out in the Human Rights Act 1998, which provides for respect for the home and non-discrimination on the grounds of sex, race, religion or 'other status',

The Inheritance (Provision for Family and Dependants) Act 1975, as amended

In broad terms the Act permits claims to a reasonable share of your estate after your death even if your will leaves the claimants nothing. Possible claimants include:

- your wife, husband or civil partner;

- your former wife, former husband or former civil partner who has not remarried or registered new civil partnership;

- your children (adopted children claim against the estate of their adoptive parents, not their birth parents);

- any person who was treated as a child of any marriage or civil partnership to which you have been a party;

- anyone who considers that he or she was maintained by you to a material extent immediately before your death. Maintenance need not be for any minimum period or financial; it can be maintenance provided in kind, e.g. by providing free food or lodgings. However, a gift of a house made several years ago is not sufficient because it is not made immediately before your death, even though the claimant may still be living in it.

A spouse or civil partner who successfully makes a claim will be awarded what is reasonable whether or not it is required for the claimant's maintenance; any other claimant can only be awarded maintenance. Payment of the claimant's debts does not constitute maintenance unless the payment enables the claimant to receive income which he would not otherwise receive or the debts are for living expenses incurred since your death.

The first question the court has to decide is whether the claimant is within the category of people authorised by the Act to make a claim.

The fact that the claimant is living in England illegally is irrelevant and the Forfeiture Act 1982 will not necessarily prevent a person who causes your demise by a criminal act from succcessfully making a claim under the Inheritance (Provision for Family and Dependants) Act 1975!

A different-sex partner and possibly a same sex partner (whether the partnership is registered or not) who has been cohabiting with you in the same household as if you were man and wife or civil partner for two years immediately prior to your death can claim without having to prove he or she was maintained by you.

If two people have been living in the same household, the fact that they are temporarily separated and not living under the same roof does not mean that they have ceased to be part of the same household if they and the public still regard them as a couple. The question to be asked is 'Is there a public and private acknowledgement of their companionship and the mutual support that binds them together?' Furthermore, what is meant by the word 'immediately' has to be construed in the light of all the surrounding circumstances and can have a wider meaning than might at first be thought. A court will not only look at the previous two-year period if previous events explain what happened during the two-year period.

The case of *Gully v Dix In re Dix deceased*, which was decided by the Court of Appeal in January 2004, is a good example. The facts were that the claimant and the deceased lived together from 1974 until August 2001 when the claimant moved out because the deceased's alcoholism caused her to fear for her safety. She never returned and in October 2001 the deceased died. Even though she had not returned before the death, as far as the claimant was concerned, the relationship was not over and the three months' separation was unusual rather than the 'settled' situation. The court decided that the important word was 'household' not 'house'. To decide whether the claimant was being maintained by the deceased and whether she and the deceased were living together in the same household immediately before his death, it was necessary to look at the reason for her leaving and the entire period during which they had been together, not just the last three months. In the light of their long-standing relationship and the reason for her leaving, in spite of the fact that she had been away from the house for the three months or so before the death, the court decided that she could be considered to be living in the same houschold as the deceased and maintained by him for the two years immediately before his death and was therefore entitled to make a claim.

The High Court or a County Court exercising matrimonial jurisdiction can bar a spouse or civil partner from making a claim under the Act on or after successful proceedings for annulment of marriage, divorce, dissolution of partnership or judicial separation.

The remaining questions to be decided are whether you have made reasonable provision for the claimant, whether or not the court should exercise the discretion the Act gives to it and, if so, to what extent.

What is a reasonable share depends upon all the circumstances of the individual case. The High Court put it rather well when it quoted with approval a Canadian judge who ruled that reasonable maintenance was enough to enable the applicant to live 'neither luxuriously, nor miserably but decently and comfortably'.

Factors which will be considered include the size of your estate, your conduct and that of the parties, the needs and resources of the parties (including those arising from mental or physical disabilities) and the length of time the relationship existed. In assessing a claimant's situation a court can hold it against him that in the past he has invested in speculative investments or lived beyond his means. You might decide that you wish to leave a statement either in your will or in a separate note stating why you have made no, or only limited, provision for a potential claimant. A specimen statement containing some reasons which might be applicable in a particular case can be found in the specimen note contained in the appendix to this book, but other reasons might be relevant and could be included. If you leave the statement in your will, remember that when probate of your will has been granted after your death the will will be a public document and anyone can obtain a copy for a nominal charge. It is usually better to leave any such statement in a separate note and keep it with your will. Such a statement no longer has any statutory effect but in the event of any claim your executors would find it useful.

It should also be noted that section 9 (1) of the Act provides that 'if a deceased person was immediately before his death beneficially entitled to a joint tenancy of any property...the court...may order that the deceased's severable share of that property...be treated...as part of the net estate of the deceased'.

Proceedings under the Act can be brought in the County Court or in the High Court, but they must be started within six months of the issue of a grant of representation to your estate unless the claimant can satisfy the court that there were exceptional reasons for the delay.

You must therefore either make reasonable provision in your will for those described above as entitled to claim against your estate or risk an expensive challenge being made to the provisions of your will.

INTANGIBLE ASSETS

Most other intangible items such as debts, patents, copyright rights, rights to sue for damages (except to sue for defamation) and contracts to which the personality of the parties is not an essential element can be left by will.

PRIVATE PENSION SCHEME BENEFITS

Private pension schemes frequently include benefits relating to death in service and benefits to take effect after the pensioner's death. Usually these matters are decided by the rules of the scheme administered by the trustees of the scheme outside the will and the beneficiaries are chosen by the trustees at their discretion, but the trustees will usually give effect to the member's intentions expressed in a statement of the member's wishes. The advantage of these provisions is that the benefits do not form part of the member's estate for the purpose of calculating inheritance tax.

Matters to Consider When Contemplating Making Your Will

JOINT WILLS

A joint will is a single document, properly completed as their wills, by two or more people who have the requisite testamentary capacity. A joint will is treated as the separate wills of those who make it and can be revoked by each party without the consent of the other or others.

I see no merit in being a party to a joint will. Do not make one. It has nothing to recommend it and is confusing and inconvenient. On the first death the original will will be retained when submitted for probate.

THE NUMBER OF EXECUTORS

Your executor is the person who is charged with the responsibility of seeing that your will is carried out. This includes arranging the funeral, taking charge of the assets, proving the will in the probate registry, paying any debts including the funeral expenses, agreeing and discharging any inheritance or other tax liability, distributing the estate to the correct beneficiaries and generally winding up your financial matters.

It is sensible to appoint at least two executors in case one should refuse the appointment or otherwise lose his physical or mental capacity before he has commenced or completed the winding up of the estate, or at least to appoint someone to be substituted as the executor to cover such an eventualities. The appointment of two executors provides an element of double checking and each can keep an eye on the other!

In the case of land or buildings it is sometimes necessary to have two executors to enable them to act. This occurs if the house or land is not sold or transferred during the course of the administration of the estate, i.e. before, or more or less at the same time as the executor has collected the assets together and paid and discharged the debts and liabilities of the estate. At that stage, in law, the executor technically ceases to be an executor and becomes a trustee.

In most cases, at that stage, the executor is in a position to sell the assets of the estate (including any land or house) or to distribute them to those entitled under the terms of the will, but sometimes the executor is unable or unwilling to sell or transfer the house or land immediately because the will contains a trust of the house or land. Examples will perhaps make the position clearer:

1. a testator who has married for a second time might give his house to be used to provide a home for his wife during the remainder of her life or until she remarries and thereafter to the children of his first marriage; or

2. a testator might leave his house to such of his children as shall attain the age of 21 and the children being under that age at the time of the testator's death, the executor might decide that it is in the interest of the potential beneficiaries to keep the house for some time as an investment for them.

The law is that in the case of a sale by a trustee, if the trustee is a trust corporation (such as a bank) or there is more than one trustee selling, a purchaser who pays the sale money to the trust corporation or to the several trustees is protected against claims by the beneficiaries of the trust that the sale is in breach of the terms of the trust. For this reason when once the administration period has ended and the executor has, in law, become a trustee, any purchaser who is properly advised will insist that he pays the purchase money either to a trust corporation or to at least two trustees and if only one executor was appointed and that executor is not a trust corporation, the executor/trustee will be compelled at that stage to incur the expense of having an additional trustee appointed to the trusts of the will to facilitate the sale.

Do not appoint more executors than necessary because probate will only be granted to the first four named executors and the greater the number of executors who prove the will, the more cumbersome the signing of withdrawal forms, receipts, deeds, etc. becomes. Personally I find two executors to be a convenient number. Co-executors have equal powers and none is senior to any other.

Separate executors can be appointed for separate parts of the estate and this can sometimes be useful if specialised knowledge is required, for example, if you have foreign property or a business.

WHOM SHOULD YOU CHOOSE TO BE YOUR EXECUTORS?

Beneficiaries can be executors, but executors need not be beneficiaries and your executors do not have to be chosen from the beneficiaries, although it might be a good idea to consider appointing a principal beneficiary as an executor. If you give legacies to your executors, the legacies can be made conditional upon the executors proving your will.

Your executors should be capable of and willing to undertake the considerable responsibilities involved and should be people who are likely to be around and have the time to do the work involved. Do not choose executors who are much older than yourself or who are likely to live a great distance away from you when you die.

It goes without saying that you should choose as your executors people you feel you can trust and believe to be scrupulously honest because they will have complete control of your assets when you are no longer alive. If possible, choose executors who are likely to receive the blessing of the beneficiaries; a good relationship between executors and beneficiaries does wonders for the smooth, speedy, efficient and financially economical management of an estate. The future happiness of your loved ones might very much depend upon your executors and the manner in which they administer your estate. Choose executors who are known to be in good health, stable, competent and reliable. Your executors should be strong characters who are not likely to be unduly influenced by any particular beneficiary in the exercise of any discretion entrusted to them.

A court has a discretion as to whether it will confirm the appointment of an executor by granting probate to him and will refuse to confirm the appointment, or replace an appointed executor by an independent executor, whenever it considers it is in the interests of the administration of the estate to do so, irrespective of any misconduct on the part of the former. In deciding whether or not to exercise its discretion the wishes of the beneficiaries will receive careful consideration.

The mentally ill can be appointed as executors, but they cannot act until they have recovered.

Minors can be appointed as executors, but they cannot act until they are of age.

Professionals (solicitors, banks or trust companies) are slow and will expect to be allowed to charge for their services (sometimes heftily). The Trustee Act 2000 provides that in the absence of an express clause in the will, a trust corporation is entitled to charge 'reasonable remuneration' for services it provides and a trustee who acts in a professional capacity, but is not a trust corporation and not a sole trustee, is entitled to charge 'reasonable remuneration' for services he provides, if every other trustee agrees in writing that he may be remunerated for his services. Trustee includes executor. These provisions do not apply to trustees of charitable trusts and are not totally satisfactory. It is better to insert an express clause in the will to deal with professional executors' fees and not rely upon the provisions of the Trustee Act.

Much of the work which professional executors do and charge for can be done equally well by a layperson, e.g. liaising with beneficiaries and estate agents, but if disputes are likely or in cases where complex assets or trusts are involved it might be advisable to appoint professionals who are knowledgeable and will not be easily influenced. Sometimes it is a good idea to appoint a member of your family, who will know the family background, to act jointly with a solicitor who will be able to supply the technical expertise. However, an appointment of the partners, or of the partners for the time being, in a named firm of solicitors or their successors in business will only be effective to appoint profit sharing partners in the firm and not salaried partners or other members of a limited liability partnership unless the appointment clause specifically makes it clear that it is intended to include them also.

To allow executors who are not trust corporations or professional trustees to charge for their services, the will must contain an express clause to that effect, otherwise they will be allowed to receive nothing more than their out-of-pocket expenses.

Above all, ask your proposed executors and make sure that they are truly willing to be executors of your will because they are not compelled to accept the position and could refuse after you are dead and unable to appoint others.

If all else fails you can appoint the Public Trustee to act as your executor, but he is not allowed to manage a charitable trust or a business or to administer an insolvent estate. As with any other executor he has the right to refuse the appointment and should be consulted in advance. His fees for acting will have to be paid out of the assets of your estate.

APPOINTING GUARDIANS FOR YOUR CHILDREN BY WILL

Guardians are people who have certain rights and responsibilities in respect of those under the age of 18. A guardian has a right to physical possession of the child (known as the ward) of whom he or she is guardian. This is useful if any attempt is made to abduct the child. The guardian also has a duty of care for the child and a duty to ensure that it is educated, but no obligation to contribute financially to the child's welfare or right to inherit from the child under the intestacy laws. A guardian is entitled to consent or refuse to the ward's adoption, marriage and medical treatment and decide upon its religion or decide that it shall have no religion.

If you have or may have a child who is under the age of 18, it is important that you should consider the appointment of a guardian for the child in your will. It is particularly important in case both parents die as a result of a common accident and in the case of single parents.

Guardianship of children is dealt with by the Children's Act 1989 as amended by the Law Reform (Succession) Act of 1995, the Adoption and Children's Act 2002 and the Civil Partnership Act 2004. To have the power to appoint a guardian by will you must have 'parental responsibility' for the child. Parental responsibility means all the rights, duties, powers, responsibilities and authority which a parent of a child has in relation to the child and the child's property by law.

The following people have parental responsibility and consequently can appoint a guardian by will:

◆ the mother and father of a child who were married to each other at the time of the child's birth;

- the child's mother whether or not she was married to the father at the time of the child's birth;

- the father of a child who was not married to the mother at the time of the child's birth but who has subsequently married the mother or been given parental responsibility by a valid parental responsibility agreement entered into with the child's mother or who has been registered as the father in England/ Scotland/Northern Ireland or Wales;

- a registered civil partner who had been granted parental responsibility in respect of the partner's partner's child;

- in relation to a child placed for adoption, the prospective adopters while the child is in their care. (The relevant Adoption Agency has parental responsibility for the child when the child is in its care.)

- a person granted parental responsibility in relation to a child by a court;

- a guardian appointed in accordance with the Act;

- a person appointed as a 'Special Guardian' by an order made under the 2002 Act. A Special Guardian is entitled to exercise parental responsibility to the exclusion of any other person except any other Special Guardian and may appoint another to be the child's guardian in the event of death of the Special Guardian. Special guardianship orders are intended to give permanence to children not considered suitable for adoption.

Unless registered in the United Kingdom as the father, the father of a child who was not married to the child's mother at the time of the child's birth does not have parental responsibilities in relation to the child merely by being the father, but a mother and father who were not married to each other at the birth of a child may enter into a written agreement in a form prescribed by the Lord Chancellor to give the father parental responsibility. The form must be registered with the Principal Registry of the Family Division of the High Court and the signatures to the form must be witnessed by a Justice of the Peace or by an official of the Registry, or County Court or Family Proceedings (Magistrates) Court. The Principal Registry of the Family Division is at the Principal Probate Registry, 42–49 High Holborn, London WC1V 6NP.

Parental responsibility ceases:

◆ if the child dies or
◆ reaches the age of 18 or
◆ is adopted or
◆ if a court removes parental responsibility.

A person who has parental responsibility or a guardian can appoint another to be the child's guardian in the event of the parent or guardian's death. The appointment must be in writing, dated and signed by the person making the appointment or (a) in the case of an appointment by will which is not signed by the testator it must be signed in the presence of and at the direction of the testator in accordance with the requirements for a valid will or (b) in any other case signed at the direction of the person making the appointment in his presence and in the presence of two witnesses who each attest the signature.

If on the death of the person making the appointment there is no person with parental responsibility for the child and no residence order in force, the appointment takes effect on the death of the person making the appointment. If on the death of the person making the appointment there is a person with parental responsibility for the child and no residence order in force, the appointment takes effect when the child no longer has anyone with parental responsibility for him.

If you appoint a guardian by your will the appointment does not displace a person with parental responsibilities or a person in favour of whom a residence order has been made and takes effect when such a person's rights have finished.

If you appoint a guardian by your will or codicil the appointment will revoke any earlier such appointment unless you make it clear that the later appointment is intended to take effect as an appointment of an additional guardian.

An appointment of a guardian by will or by codicil can be terminated:

- by a court;

- by revocation of the will or codicil;

- by a dated document made by the person who made the appointment, which document is signed by the maker or signed at his direction, in his presence and in the presence of two witnesses who each attest the signature.

A written appointment of a guardian made otherwise than by a will or codicil can be terminated:

◆ by a court;

◆ by a dated document which is signed by the maker or signed at his direction, in his presence and in the presence of two witnesses who each attest the signature;

◆ if to take effect on death by the person who made the appointment destroying the document by which it was made with the intention of revoking it or having some other person destroy it in his presence.

A written appointment of a spouse or civil partner to be a guardian, whether or not by will or codicil, is also revoked by a divorce or annulment or dissolution as the case may be which is recognised by the laws of England and Wales, unless the document which makes the appointment shows a contrary intention.

A person appointed as guardian is not obliged to accept the appointment and is entitled to disclaim the appointment in a signed written document within a reasonable time of learning that the appointment has taken effect; you should therefore obtain the agreement of the person concerned before appointing him to be the guardian of your child.

In your will you will need to consider providing for your children's maintenance. Guardians have no right to be reimbursed for anything they spend in bringing up your children unless you give them such a right by your will. You should also consider carefully whether or not the guardians should also be executors of the will and whether or not they should be the sole executors. In the absence of a clause in your will which expressly permits it, the law permits executors to use only up to one half of the capital bequeathed to a minor for the minor's benefit and if your estate is small your will should contain a clause which increases the proportion. In the case of a bequest to any under-age beneficiary, whether or not the beneficiary is your child, if the guardians are not the only executors, your will should contain a clause which authorises your executors, in their discretion, to pay money to the guardians for the minor's benefit and for the guardians to give the executors a valid receipt and discharge for any money which is paid to the guardians. Under-age beneficiaries have no power in law to give valid receipts or discharges for capital and only minors who are married can give a receipt for income.

YOUR FUNERAL AND THE DISPOSAL OF YOUR BODY AFTER YOUR DEATH

If you leave a will your executors are entitled to claim your body and have the right and duty to dispose of it and arrange the funeral. If you do not leave a will the person primarily entitled to obtain a grant of letters of administration of the estate on your intestacy is the person entitled to these rights. (See pages 7–9 to decide who that person is.) What happens if there are several people equally entitled who wish to deal with the disposal of your body or your funeral in different ways? An application can be made to a judge of the Chancery Division of the High Court to decide the matter using his judicial discretion. The principal guideline used by a judge in deciding the matter is that your body must be treated with proper respect and decency and with as little delay as possible. If one person has already made proper arrangements, for practical reasons that person's wishes will often be preferred. Subsidiary factors the judge will take into account are the wishes you held or might be expected to have held and the reasonable views of your family and friends.

Although in law the right to decide upon matters relating to your funeral and the disposal of your body is that of your personal representatives it is usual to insert a clause in your will to set out your wishes in relation to these matters. Such a clause will guide your executors who will usually comply with them as far as they are able. The clause should be kept as brief as possible.

The chances of your executors complying with your wishes can perhaps be strengthened by leaving a legacy to your executors which is made conditional upon your wishes being carried out, as long as your wishes are not unlawful!

If your body is not claimed the local authority will dispose of it, as far as possible at the expense of the estate. If the local authority disposes of your body it is not permitted to cause your body to be cremated if it has reason to believe that to do so would be contrary to your wishes.

The following notes might be of assistance when considering how you would like your body to be disposed of after your death.

If you intended to have your funeral out of England and Wales (for example in Scotland), the coroner's permission will have to be obtained at the appropriate time to take your body out of England or Wales, whether or not it has been necessary to report the death to the coroner, and you might wish to bear this in mind when leaving directions in your will for your funeral.

If you wish your body to be cremated, cremation can only take place at an authorised crematorium, but your ashes can be buried or scattered on your land or the land of another with the owner's permission or scattered at sea.

Another possibility is to have them buried in the Garden of Remembrance of the crematorium where cremation takes place or of another crematorium. Many crematoria no longer permit the scattering of ashes in the Remembrance Garden or the burial of containers; the ashes are buried directly into the soil.

Some churchyards and cemeteries have areas for the burial of cremated remains and may permit them to be buried in a container even if they are full for burial of non-cremated remains. Burial of the ashes in a family grave which is considered to be full for the purpose of non-cremated remains is sometimes permitted.

If you wish to be buried in a churchyard or cemetery and are keen to have a particular type of headstone or memorial, check that the proposed burial ground is not likely to object to the type of headstone or other memorial that you have in mind, because churches and municipal cemetery proprietors are becoming increasingly fussy as to what they will allow. 'Green' funerals in woodland burial grounds are becoming increasingly popular and the Natural Death Centre, In The Hill House, Watley Lane, Twyford, Winchester, SO21 1QX, tel: 0871 288 2098, fax: 020 7354 3831, website: *www.naturaldeath.org.uk*, can supply useful information about these funerals.

Although burial does not have to take place in a churchyard or cemetery, it must not constitute a danger to public health or pose a pollution threat to the water supply and if you wish to be buried anywhere but in a churchyard or a cemetery, it is as well to check first that the local and water authorities have no objection. The Ministry of Justice is able to advise. If you proposed to be buried in your garden careful thought should be given to the resale value of the property and the problem of tending the grave if the property is sold at a future date. You should also check your title deeds to ensure that they do not contain restrictions on the use of the property that prevent its use for burial purposes. Your executors will need to keep a record of the site of the burial with the title deeds because it is illegal to disturb a grave without permission from the Ministry of Justice. The date and place of the burial will also have to be notified to the Registrar of Deaths within 96 hours of the burial. Your burial must not disturb a recognised archaeological site and any grave marker, high fencing or wall or multiple burials might require planning permission.

Burial at sea can be arranged with the assistance of a professional funeral director. It is authorised by the Food and Environment Protection Act 1985 and a licence from the Marine and Fisheries Agency (which is a section of the Department of the Environment, Farming and Rural Affairs) and a special coffin will be required. The Agency can be contacted through its local offices, the addresses of which are given on its website at *www.mfa.gov.uk/contact/local.htm*. The licence, if granted, is given by letter and is free of charge. Burial at sea is not permitted if the body has been embalmed and a certificate from a medical practitioner to the effect that the body is free from fever or infection must accompany the application for a licence. It can only take place in certain parts of the sea and the coroner's permission will be required to take your body out of the country. Such burials are expensive.

No licence is required to scatter ashes at sea.

If you wish your body to be used for organ transplants it is as well to let your family know, register on the NHS Organ Donor Register and carry a donor card because organs have to be removed within a few hours of death if they are to be of use. Donor cards are available from doctors and pharmacies. The NHS Organ Donor Register's address is UK Transplant, Fox Den Road, Stoke Gifford, Bristol BS34 8RR. Tel: 0300 123 2323. Website: *uktransplant.org.uk*

MAKING PROVISION FOR YOUR PETS

If you have a pet or pets you will need to consider expressing your wishes for them if they are still alive when you die in your will.

You can leave them by will to a trusted friend or relative and you should note that a bequest of 'my personal chattels' would include your domestic animals. However, before bequeathing pets make sure that the friend or relative who is to receive them is happy to do so and able to accept the responsibility of caring for them. If you bequeath a pet to a friend or relative it is only fair that provision should also be made for its upkeep. A direct legacy to your pet cannot be easily enforced because your pet cannot itself sue for the legacy! A bequest of £x per annum to be paid to a friend out of the residue of your estate on condition the friend takes good care of the pet during its lifetime might both be more effective and perhaps extend the life of the pet!

If you have no friend or relative who is likely to survive you and be happy and able to care for your pets, the RSPCA have a 'Home for Life' service which will endeavour to re-home pets to a suitable, caring new home. The RSPCA do ask that you notify them of your intention to include a clause assigning your pets to them in your will, because this makes it absolutely clear that they have ownership of the animal. In order to avoid any doubt, the RSPCA would ideally like to have a copy of the will which it states will be kept absolutely confidential. A 'Home for Life' registration form is available at *www.homeforlife.org.uk* or can be obtained by telephoning the RSPCA on 0300 1234 555 or by post from RSPCA Freepost SEA1050 03, Horsham RH13 9RS. Confirmation of registration will be sent to you once the RSPCA know that the relevant clause has been added to the will and they have the details of the pets.

The Blue Cross operates a similar scheme limited to up to four dogs, cats and small furry animals. Fish and exotic species are not accepted and details of their scheme can be obtained from their website *www.bluecross.org.uk*, by post from The Blue Cross, Freepost OF224, Room L335, Shilton Road, Burford, Oxon, OX18 4PF or by telephoning 01993 825594.

The Dogs Trust has a re-homing scheme for dogs and details can be obtained from 17 Wakeley Street, London EC1V 7RQ or by telephoning 020 7837 0006 between 9.00 a.m and 5.00 p.m. on Mondays to Fridays or from its website (*www.dogstrust.org.uk*).

While these organisations appreciate legacies for their general work, none of them insists upon one being given.

THE USE OF TRUSTS IN YOUR WILL

Trusts can be set up in your will to last for a maximum of 80 years and the income from trust funds accumulated for a maximum of 21 years.

Interest in possession trusts and their uses

Interest in possession trusts are trusts in which someone or some organisation (technically known as the life tenant or tenant for life), has a present or immediate legal entitlement to benefit from the trust fund for his life or any other limited time (the interest in possession), after which the benefit will pass to another person. The purpose of an interest in possession trust is to provide income or the benefit of the trust assets for a beneficiary for a limited period whilst preserving the assets of the trust, i.e. the capital of the trust, for the subsequent benefit or use of others.

You will find an interest in possession trust particularly useful if you have a second or subsequent marriages or civil partnership and wish your assets to benefit your spouse/partner after your death but to ensure that they are inherited by your children and no one else after her death. For example, you might leave your house to trustees upon trust to provide a home for your widow during the remainder of her life and to be inherited by your children after her death. In this way you are able to provide for your widow, but at the same time to extend the period during which you can control the destiny of your asset.

Interest in possession trusts are also useful to provide for the maintenance of individual children until they are capable of providing for themselves. They are expensive from an income tax point of view if the income exceeds £100 per annum and the trust

funds have been provide by a parent, as opposed to say by a
grandparent, because in the former event (for income tax
purposes) the income will be considered to be that of the parent
and the child will not be able to set his personal tax-free income
tax allowances against the income.

Relevant property or discretionary trusts and their uses

A relevant property trust is a trust in respect of which no
individual beneficiary has a present or immediate right to a
defined part of the trust assets or of the income of the trust
during the life of the trust: during the life of the trust the trustees
have a discretion to divide them as they think fit between any one
or more beneficiaries (or class or classes of beneficiaries) specified
in the trust deed. For this reason relevant property trusts are
frequently referred to as discretionary trusts. Until the trustees
have made a decision and exercised their discretion, all the
individual potential beneficiaries have is a hope or expectation of
benefiting from the trust even though, in accordance with the
general principles of trust law, if the potential beneficiaries all
have full legal capacity they can collectively put an end to the
trust and share the trust funds between them.

If you leave assets on a discretionary trust it is usual to leave a
letter of wishes stating the principles you wish the trustees to use
when deciding how to exercise the discretion you have given them
concerning the allocation of the trust fund and the income it
produces. If you leave a letter of wishes great care must be taken
in the drafting of the letter to ensure that the trustees' discretion
remains legally unfettered and that they are free to ignore your
wishes, otherwise the trust will be classed as an interest in
possession trust and not as a discretionary trust.

The principal advantage of a discretionary trust is that no inheritance tax is charged upon the death of a potential beneficiary because no beneficiary has a right to any defined interest in the trust assets or the income they produce until the trustees have exercised their discretion in his favour.

A further major benefit of discretionary trusts is flexibility. Within the wide boundaries set out in the trust deed a discretionary trust permits the trustees to use the trust fund in the way they consider to be most appropriate having regard to the circumstances which exist at the times they make their decisions. The circumstances at these times might be very different from those that existed at the time you set up the trust and considered your objectives.

Discretionary trusts are frequently used to provide for people whose financial needs are likely to vary at different times in the future or to protect the trust fund from creditors if one of the potential beneficiaries is a spendthrift or engaged in hazardous business ventures and likely to become bankrupt.

Section 144 of the Inheritance Tax Act 1984 contains a provision which is especially useful if you are apt to be tardy in reviewing your will when tax law or your circumstances change. This section facilitates what is commonly referred to as a two-year discretionary trust. In effect it provides that if a discretionary trust is created in your will, transfers made out of the trust not less than three months and not more than two years after your death can be treated as being dispositions made in the will and directly made by you. In practice it allows your trustees to change your will within the prescribed time limits after your death to take advantage of changes in circumstances without incurring additional inheritance tax. It should be noted that if trustees of a two-year discretionary will trust use their discretion to allocate capital and choose that the allocation shall be considered as having been made by you in your will, the recipient will be considered to acquire the allocated assets for the purposes of capital gains tax at the base value which exists at the date of the allocation and not that which existed at the date of your death. Any gain or loss in the value of the relevant trust asset between the date of your death and the date of the allocation will be considered to be that of the trust for capital gains tax purposes.

Quite apart from section 144 any discretionary trust can contain a clause permitting the trustees to add to the list of potential beneficiaries and such a clause could prove to be a cheap way of settling claims made under the Inheritance (Provision for Family and Dependants) Act 1975.

Inheritance tax on trusts set up in your will
This subject is dealt with in Chapter 5, pages 104–107 and further and more detailed information concerning inheritance tax can be found in my book *How to save inheritance tax*.

MATTERS TO CONSIDER WHICH MIGHT INFLUENCE YOUR CHOICE OF BENEFICIARIES

Your family and dependants
I have already mentioned the Inheritance (Provision for Family and Dependants) Act 1975 in Chapter 3 and to avoid a possible challenge to your will you might consider making reasonable provision for anyone who is in a position to have a reasonable chance of making a successful claim.

Elderly beneficiaries

If your principal beneficiaries are elderly, ask yourself how much they need in addition to what they already have in their own name. There will be a limit to how much they can spend to improve the quality of their lives if they only have a short time left to them and if they leave a large estate your bequest might aggravate their inheritance tax problem. Might it be better to skip a generation and save inheritance tax? At the other end of the scale consider the effect of your bequests upon beneficiaries' social security benefits.

The family home

I advise that you endeavour to keep a roof over your partner's or spouse's head irrespective of the effect it will have on inheritance tax on her death. Too often have I seen a child whose business has got into financial difficulties decide that it would be better for Mum to pass the family home to him to avoid inheritance tax on her death and incidentally allow him to use it as collateral security for a loan to support a failing business. It is not worth taking the risk that your spouse could be made homeless merely to save inheritance tax and any spouse who is reasonably able to care for herself should be given independence and security by being left the home rather than having to rely upon the goodwill of the family.

If you wish to make gifts while you are still alive in an effort to reduce the amount of inheritance tax payable on your death and you have insufficient liquid assets because your wealth is tied up in your home, you must bear in mind the rules relating to gifts with a reservation of an interest and the income tax charge on the use of pre-owned assets. Both of these concepts are dealt with in the next chapter. Possible solutions which you might wish to consider are to 'downsize', or to raise money upon the security of the home by means of an equity release scheme such as a roll up mortgage or a home reversionary scheme.

Downsizing is to sell your property and to move into a cheaper property. A roll up mortgage is a mortgage in respect of which you are not required to make repayments until you sell the property or die. In a home reversionary scheme you sell part or the entirety of the family home or borrow against it and in either case on the understanding that you are allowed to remain in it until you sell it or you either go into long-term care or die. If you are married or have a partner, the property should be jointly owned and the roll up mortgage or equity release scheme should be entered into jointly so that the survivor of you will have the benefits.

If you propose to enter into any of these schemes you should check:

◆ that you will be able to sell and move into another suitable property without terminating the scheme if, as a result of a change in your circumstances, your existing property becomes unsuitable;

◆ whether you will incur any and if so what penalty charge if you wish to terminate the scheme early for any reason;

◆ that there is a guarantee that you (or your estate when you die) will not be required to make up any deficiency if the value of the property becomes lower than the outstanding debt; and

◆ what effect any income you receive from the scheme or from investing any capital you obtain will have on your income tax position or means tested benefits.

You should also remember that entering into an equity release scheme would possibly prevent a third party, such as a daughter or other carer, living with you. If it did not do so it would almost certainly necessitate them leaving and perhaps becoming homeless when the scheme terminated upon your death or when it became necessary to enter into care. Throughout the entire period of the scheme or of a roll up mortgage, you would remain responsible for paying council tax and maintaining and insuring the property.

If you give away cash you received under an equity release scheme it could possibly affect the chances of having care home fees paid for you in the future.

It is essential to obtain independent legal and financial advice before entering into any such arrangements and to note that legal and surveyor's fees will be charged, although some, but not all, companies will reimburse the fees if the scheme is completed.

Gifts to the young and age-contingent gifts
Are your younger beneficiaries able to handle large sums of money sensibly or should bequests to them be held on trust for them until they reach a specified age? If so, what age, and who should hold it for them, your executors or their parents? Are the parents under the influence of the children and will they give way to the children's wishes under pressure? Should the trustees be empowered in their discretion to use the income and/or the capital for the children before they reach the specified age and if so how much of the capital or income? Should use for the children be limited to use for specified purposes for them, for example for their education? The answers to these questions depend to a large extent upon the individuals concerned, but in reaching a decision there are some legal and some tax points to be borne in mind.

There is a statutory power, which can be expressly excluded or enlarged by your will, for trustees (which includes executors) to pay or apply for the benefit of minors or beneficiaries who are contingently entitled under a trust (including a will) up to one half of the capital of the funds to which they are contingently entitled. There is also a statutory power for trustees to use the income of a bequest in this way, but it is much more complicated and does not apply to all kinds of bequests. In the case of income it is better to include an express power to use the income in this way if that is what you wish.

If a bequest produces income which is not given to or used for the benefit of the beneficiary in a particular tax year (for example because the will gives it to the beneficiary only if the beneficiary fulfils a particular condition which has not yet been fulfilled and the executors do not exercise any discretion they may have to so use it), the income is added to the capital of the bequest and incurs income tax at the rate applicable to trusts (40% in general or 32.5% for dividend income).

Trusts for bereaved minors and trusts for the disabled operate under a different scheme and are taxed at the rate applicable to the beneficiary (not at the trust rate) and are able to use the beneficiary's personal tax allowances.

Remember that each trust and each person has capital gains tax allowances and every individual, irrespective of their age, has income tax allowances which allow them to have limited capital gains and income free of tax. If the executors invest the accumulated income and they later sell the investments at a profit, the net profit will be counted as the trust's gain for capital gains tax purposes and set against the trust's capital gains tax exemption. Moreover, income cannot be legally allowed to accumulate indefinitely and accumulations must cease within 21 years of your death.

The income from a bequest is small compared with the capital of the bequest and I consider that the best solution to overcome these problems is to leave bequests to young beneficiaries in such a way that they only inherit the capital of the bequest when they reach an age when they can be expected to be as sensible as they ever will be, and to provide that they shall be entitled to the income irrespective of their age at the time of your death, for example to say 'I leave the sum of £x to my trustees to pay or apply the income thereof for the benefit of Y absolutely irrespective of his age and as to the capital thereof for Y if he shall attain the age of 21 years'. Even if the bequest is left in this way, any capital gains which arise from the sale of investments in which the trustees invest the capital representing the legacy pending Y reaching the age of 21 will be added to any capital gains made on the disposal of any other investments made by the trustees, for example gains made on the realisation by the trustees of any investments in which the trustees have invested the funds of other bequests which are still contingent, and the gains will count towards the trust's capital gains exemption limit.

What age should you choose for a contingent gift to become an absolute one? Again this depends in part upon the people concerned and their individual circumstances, but there is a rule of law that forbids bequests under which it is not possible to ascertain for an excessively long time who is to inherit the gift. The rule is

known as the rule against perpetuities and its application is
complex. It is safer to make sure that any gifts in your will are
confined to people who will be born and ascertained within 21
years of your death, and not to make gifts to anyone who will not,
within 21 years from your death, inevitably fulfil any condition
necessary to qualify.

When deciding upon the allocation of your various assets between
the various beneficiaries, consider giving the assets with the
greatest growth potential to younger rather than older individuals
because in the normal course of things they will have longer to
live before inheritance tax is payable on the recipient's death.

Whenever you make bequests to minors in your will you will need
to include a specific clause in your will to authorise someone to
give a receipt and a good discharge to your executors for anything
they pay or transfer to or for the benefit of the minor, because the
law does not permit an under-age person to give a valid receipt or
discharge. It is usual to provide that a parent or guardian may
give the receipt and discharge and a specimen clause is provided
in the appendix to this book.

Bequests to spendthrifts and bankrupts

When a person becomes bankrupt, most of his assets are taken by
his trustee in bankruptcy to be used to settle his debts. If one of
your chosen beneficiaries is bankrupt when you die, as much of
your bequest as is necessary will be used for the benefit of the
creditors and not for the beneficiary. Consequently, if one of your
chosen beneficiaries is a spendthrift and likely to become
bankrupt, you might decide it to better to leave your bequest to
his close family rather than to him.

Although any attempt to impose a condition on a gift that the gift shall be forfeited if the beneficiary becomes bankrupt will be ineffective and the bequest will take effect free from the condition and pass to the beneficiary's trustee in bankruptcy for the benefit of the creditors, it is possible to give something to a beneficiary *until* he becomes bankrupt and then to someone else. The difference is between making an absolute gift and then taking it back if bankruptcy occurs and making a gift for a limited period until bankruptcy occurs.

A variation is to leave the gift to your executors or separate trustees on discretionary trusts, such as to pay the income to such members of a group of named people, including the spendthrift, as the trustees shall in their discretion decide until the spendthrift beneficiary becomes bankrupt or dies, whichever shall happen first and then to pass the capital to another named beneficiary or beneficiaries. Such an arrangement would not guarantee that the spendthrift would get anything, but neither would his trustee in bankruptcy.

Yet a further possible solution is to leave the bequest on what is known as a protective trust. This means that you would leave the bequest to your executors or to separate trustees, upon trust to pay the income of the bequest to your chosen beneficiary until he becomes bankrupt or dies, whichever shall happen first and then to such members of a group of named beneficiaries (which could include the spendthrift), in such proportions as the trustees shall in their discretion decide.

There is a statutory form of protective trust, the terms of which are set out in section 33 of the Trustee Act 1925 and which can be incorporated in your will by stating that the gift is to be held upon protective trusts as provided for in that section for your named beneficiary during his life or for such lesser period as you choose and state. In essence the statutory trust would ensure that if the beneficiary did anything which would deprive him of the income from the gift, e.g. if he became bankrupt, the income would be held by the trustees during his life or the lesser period for such of the named beneficiary and his spouse, children and issue (or if he had none, for such of the named beneficiary and the persons who would be entitled to the income or trust property if he were dead), as the trustees should decide.

If you use a protective trust in your will, you do of course need to state who shall have the capital of the gift after the chosen period ends.

The disadvantage of these trusts is that they are only suitable for larger bequests because it is expensive to set them up and to run them, in that running them involves investments, accounts and tax returns, and they are complicated to draft and should be drawn up by an experienced professional.

Bequests to those incapable of managing their affairs or suffering from other disabilities

If a proposed beneficiary is incapable of managing his affairs, then, unless before he became incapable he gave an enduring power of attorney before 1 October 2007 or a lasting power of attorney after that date and in either case appointing an attorney to deal with them for him, it will be necessary for a receiver or a deputy to manage them (including your bequest) for him under the supervision of the Court of Protection and Public Guardianship Office. This may not be what you wish.

An alternative solution is to leave the bequest upon a discretionary trust similar to the protective trust mentioned above in connection with spendthrift beneficiaries. Such a trust may also be useful for intended beneficiaries with other handicaps or disabilities. Your chosen trustees would be given the bequest upon trust to pay the income of the bequest during the handicapped person's lifetime to a group of named beneficiaries including the handicapped person, or to accumulate it and add it to the capital and in such proportions as the trustees in their discretion decide. The discretion given to the trustees enables them to adjust payments within limits according to the beneficiary's needs and the financial limits for any social security benefits the beneficiary might be receiving. Your will would also need to say what is to happen to any capital which is left on the handicapped beneficiary's death.

The Finance Act 2004 provides that trusts for 'the vulnerable' (minors who have at least one deceased parent and the disabled) can elect on a specified Inland Revenue form to be taxed at the rates applicable to the individual beneficiaries rather than at the (usually higher) rate for trusts. To qualify for such treatment the income must be paid to or for the use of the beneficiary by 31 December following the end of the tax year in which the income arose to the trustees. Such trusts can also use the beneficiaries' personal tax allowances and the scheme applies to both capital gains tax and income tax. To qualify as disabled for the purposes of the scheme a beneficiary must be either:

◆ unable to administer his or her property or manage his or her affairs because of mental disorder; or

♦ in receipt of either attendance allowance or disability living allowance, by virtue of entitlement to the care component at the highest or middle rate.

This scheme for taxation of the vulnerable does not apply to those trusts in which the document which creates the trust contains an express power for the trustees to advance capital from the trust to a beneficiary who will or might be entitled to it at a later date, as opposed to trusts which need to rely upon the statutory power contained in section 32 of the Trustee Act 1925.

Further guidance on the details of the scheme is contained in Guidance Notes issued by the Revenue and the Trusts, Settlements and Estates Manual and the Capital Gains Manual, which are available on the HM Revenue and Customs' website (*www.hmrc.gov.uk*).

AVOIDING CHALLENGES TO YOUR WILL

Taking precautions against fraud
Please refer to the suggestions I have made in Chapter 2 page 27.

Duress and undue influence
To be valid and enforceable your will must state your true wishes, freely considered and decided upon without pressure, influence or encouragement by any other person. You may be eccentric and your wishes may be capricious and morally unfair but if they are your own wishes, decided upon in this way, not illegal or against public policy and clearly expressed in a properly created will, they will be respected and enforced by the law.

If your will has been made under pressure or undue influence it will not be a valid will and can be set aside by a court. Evidence of undue influence may be given to a court or the court can presume undue influence from the circumstances surrounding the making of the will.

A rebuttable presumption of undue influence will arise if:

◆ the relationship you have with the beneficiary is such that you might be expected to place special trust and confidence in him. Such relationships include parent and child, guardian and ward, doctor and patient, solicitor and client and religious adviser and follower; and

◆ there are circumstances in respect of the bequest (such as its size in relation to the your estate) which make it unusual and one which would not normally be expected without an explanation.

A presumption of undue influence can be rebutted by producing evidence that in fact there was none and if you leave a note with your will to explain why you make any bequest which you feel might be challenged on the grounds of undue influence your executors might find it useful.

Your capacity to make a will
In Chapter 2 I explained the degree of understanding that the law requires a testator to have if his will is to be valid and legally enforceable. If you think that your will is likely to be challenged on the grounds that you do not have the required understanding, I

suggest that you consult your doctor and arrange for the doctor and/or a solicitor to witness your will and either to make a note in their files of their assessment of your mental capacity or to give you a letter that sets out their conclusions to place with the will.

Your beneficiaries

I have already mentioned the Inheritance (Provision for Family and Dependants) Act 1975 in Chapter 3 and you might think you wish to make reasonable provision for anyone who is in a position to have a reasonable chance of making a successful claim. Alternatively you might wish to leave a note based on the specimen note set out in the appendix to this book with your will to explain why you have made little or no provision for such a beneficiary.

5

Inheritance Tax in General

HOW INHERITANCE TAX WORKS

The previous chapter which dealt with gifts to the young and age contingent gifts touched upon the different tax consequences of leaving bequests to young people in different ways and there are other ways in which the tax payable by your family can be increased or decreased by your will. When making a will you should consider your family's position overall and as a single entity.

The main tax involved with death is inheritance tax and you need to have a basic understanding of how inheritance tax works and how it is calculated, to enable you to decide if you can take steps by your will to minimise it.

In essence, inheritance tax is a tax on gifts, whether they are made during your lifetime or whether they occur as the result of your death. It is charged whenever a gratuitous transfer of any wealth diminishes your wealth unless legislation specifies the transfer or the property transferred to be exempt. The tax payable is less if certain 'reliefs' notionally reduce either the value of the property or the tax itself.

Which of your assets are taxed?

If you have your domicile in the United Kingdom inheritance tax applies to all your non-exempt assets in whatever country they may be, but if your domicile is outside the United Kingdom the tax will only apply to those of your non-exempt assets that are situated in the United Kingdom. The United Kingdom for the purpose of inheritance tax includes England, Wales, Scotland and Northern Ireland but does not include the Channel Islands or the Isle of Man. Please refer to Chapter 3, pages 28 and 29 for an explanation of the meaning of 'domicile' and where you are deemed to be domiciled for the purposes of inheritance tax.

How the tax is calculated

Unless it is 'excluded property', upon your death inheritance tax is charged upon the total of

◆ the market value at the date of your death of everything you own and everything you have given away in the last seven years of your life which is not specifically exempted from the tax.

(A list of excluded property and a list of exempt gifts is set out on pages 82–87.)

◆ The full capital value of the assets of any trust created before 22 March 2006 of which you are entitled to the income or a share of the income for your life; such an entitlement to income is called 'a life tenancy';

◆ the full capital value of the assets of any trust created by a will or intestacy of which you are entitled to a life tenancy and which entitlement began immediately upon the death or follows immediately upon a life tenancy in existence on 6 April 2006 that ended before 6 April 2008;

◆ the full capital value of the assets of any trust of which you are entitled to a life tenancy if your entitlement follows immediately on that of your spouse or civil partner who was a life tenant of the trust on 6 April 2006 and who died on or after 6 April 2008;

◆ the full capital value of any trust of a life policy or policies created before 22 March 2006 of which you are the first or a subsequent life tenant, provided there has been no break in the sequence of life tenants;

◆ the full value of the assets of any trust which qualifies as a disablement trust under section 89 of the Inheritance Tax Act 1984 (see pages 75 and 76) and of which you are the disabled beneficiary; and

◆ the value of anything you have purported to give away at any time but from which you continued to benefit in the seven years immediately preceding your death.

You may deduct from the total of these figures:

a) the cost of realising or administering any property outside the United Kingdom up to 50% of its value;
b) your reasonable funeral expenses;
c) any debts and liabilities you have at the date of your death, but not the inheritance tax payable as a result of your death;
(d) any legacies you bequeath which are exempt legacies; and
(e) your unused nil-rate band.

The tax is calculated as a percentage of the resultant figure. The nil-rate band is the value of your estate that falls between nil and the tax threshold and is currently £325,000. The percentage for the tax year 2009/10 is 40%.

Some relief from inheritance tax is given in respect of the following assets if they have been owned for two years or more prior to death:

◆ most shares traded on the Alternative Investment Market (AIM);

◆ the agricultural value of agricultural property;

◆ businesses (other than property and investment businesses); and

◆ woodlands.

Conditional relief may also be available in respect of Heritage Assets.

Which assets are exempt from the tax?
The following are excluded property:

◆ Savings Certificates and Premium Bonds owned by people who are domiciled in the Channel Islands or the Isle of Man;

◆ certain British government stock owned by those living abroad;

◆ certain overseas pensions and lump sums payable on your death;

◆ emoluments and tangible movable property which is owned by visiting armed forces;

◆ property of service people who die as a result of active military service or from a pre-existing disease aggravated by military

- by concession, awards for valour or gallantry (not necessarily in a military context), which have never been transferred in return for money or money's worth. The award need not have remained in the same family and need not have been a medal but could be a sword or silverware for example;

- property situated outside the United Kingdom if you are domiciled outside the United Kingdom;

- your foreign currency bank accounts with most banks in the United Kingdom if you are of foreign domicile and not resident or ordinarily resident in the United Kingdom;

- most reversionary interests, i.e. most presently owned rights you have to property upon the death of someone who is currently entitled to the property during their lifetime under a trust. As an example consider the following: A by his will left his house on trust for B during B's life and after B's death for you. After A's death B would have a life interest in the house and be known as the tenant for life and you would have a reversionary interest in the house and be known as the remainderman. Reversionary interests are excluded property unless they are rights to which the person who set up the trust or his spouse or civil partner is or has been entitled or they have been acquired at any time for money or money's worth (e.g. by exchange for something which could have been sold).

Gifts which are exempt from the tax

The following gifts are exempt from inheritance tax.

- Out and out gifts you make more than seven years prior to your death without retaining any benefit from the gift, unless the gift is made to a company or to a trust (other than a trust for the disabled). Gifts you make to a company or to a trust (other than a trust for the disabled) are immediately chargeable gifts. With the exception of immediately chargeable gifts, gifts remain only potentially liable to inheritance tax for the seven years after they have been made and are known as PETS, a concept and an acronym which should be remembered because they will feature prominently in later pages. If you survive the making of a PET by seven years the PET becomes completely exempt from the tax whatever its value but because of the principle of cumulation a gift made up to 14 years before your death can affect the amount of tax payable in respect of a chargeable gift. The principle of cumulation is that chargeable transfers made within the seven year period prior to a chargeable transfer are taken into account when calculating the tax on the presently made chargeable transfer, whether those chargeable transfers are immediately chargeable lifetime transfers or potentially exempt transfers which have become chargeable as a result of the transferor's death occurring within the following seven years.

◆ Gifts of any amount you make to your spouse or registered civil partner, unless you are domiciled in the United Kingdom but your spouse or civil partner is not, in which case the exemption is limited to £55,000. It is important to remember that the survivor exemption only applies to those who are legally married and those who have registered a civil partnership. It does not apply to other cohabitees no matter how long they have been living together. The Grand Chamber of the European Court has confirmed that the rule does not infringe the right to family life recognised by The European Convention on Human Rights or The Human Rights Act.

Marriage and civil partnership involve the voluntary adoption of a body of legally recognised rights and obligations which clearly distinguish them from other forms of cohabitation.

◆ Gifts of not more than £3,000 in total which you make in any tax year. Any unused benefit from this exemption can be carried forward for one, but only one, tax year and the annual exemption for any current tax year is used up before the unused balance of the annual exemption from any previous tax year. Suppose, therefore, that you make a gift of £1,000 to your son in tax year 1 and a gift of £4,000 to your daughter in year 2. In tax year one the £1,000 gift is exempt because it is less than the £3,000 exemption level and there is £2,000 of the exemption for year 1 that can be carried forward to tax year 2. In tax year 2 the benefit of the £2,000 unused exemption from year 1 is available, together with the £3,000 annual exemption for year 2, to be set against the gift of £4,000 made to your daughter in year 2 with the result that that gift is also completely exempt, but the rule is that the excess of £2,000 from year 1 is to be used up *after* the £3,000 annual exemption for current year 2 has been applied and accordingly only £1,000 of the excess from year 1 is used in year 2. Because it can only be carried forward for one year, £1,000 of the £2,000 unused from the exemption in year 1 is wasted and cannot be used against any gift of over £3,000 made in tax year 3.

If the total value of gifts which are not covered by any other exemption in any tax year exceed this annual exemption and any useable balance from any previous tax year, the excess is taxable.

◆ Gifts made during your life which are made as part of your normal expenditure out of your income and not from capital and which do not reduce your standard of living. Normal expenditure is expenditure which is in accordance with a settled pattern of your expenditure and that pattern may be proved either by showing that you have made such payments regularly in the past or that you have taken a decision to make them in the future, for example, by entering into a covenant to do so. There is no minimum period during which the payments must be made as long as the period is more than nominal and a single payment will be sufficient if there is sufficient evidence to show that you intended to continue them.

If a gift fails exemption as a PET because you die too soon your personal representatives should check whether the gift might escape tax under this heading. The onus of claiming the exemption is upon the personal representatives.

◆ Wedding gifts made before the ceremony during your life, up to £5,000 to your child, up to £2,500 to your grandchild and up to £1,000 to anyone else.

◆ Gifts made in your lifetime for the maintenance of your spouse, ex-spouse, civil partner, ex-civil partner, or dependant relatives and dependant children who are under the age of 18 or are in full-time education.

◆ Gifts to registered charities for charitable purposes.

◆ Gifts for certain national purposes including gifts to most museums and art galleries and to political parties which have at least two sitting members of the House of Commons or which have one sitting member and whose candidates polled 150,000 votes at the last general election.

◆ Gifts of land to registered Housing Associations.

You can make gifts in any number of the above classes to the same person without losing the benefit of the exemption and, in addition, under what is known as the small gifts exemption, you can make any number of gifts of up to £250 in a tax year provided that you have made no other gift to the same person in the same tax year. If the sum you give under the small gifts exemption exceeds £250 the benefit of the exemption is lost and the entire sum is taxable. This is in contrast to the situation in respect of the annual exemption where only the excess over the amount of the exemption is taxable and the remainder is exempt.

If you are married or have a registered civil partner you should remember that each spouse and civil partner has a separate set of gift exemptions.

How the tax on gifts is calculated

The valuation of gifts
Gifts are valued for inheritance tax purposes at the amount by which your estate is diminished as a result of the gift and not by the amount by which the donee benefits from the gift. Inheritance Tax at 20% will have been paid on immediately chargeable non-exempt gifts made in your lifetime if the total value of the gifts in the previous seven years exceeded the then tax threshold and you will be given credit on your death for tax which has been paid on them, but if the tax paid exceeds the tax payable on them at death, the excess is not repayable. As mentioned above, immediately chargeable gifts are gifts to discretionary trusts and gifts to companies. Currently, inheritance tax is charged on chargeable gifts made in your lifetime at 20%, one half of the rate charged in respect of your chargeable estate at your death.

The inheritance tax threshold is £325,000 for the tax year 2009/ 2010 and the amount of your estate that falls between nil and the tax threshold is known as the *nil-rate band.* Inheritance tax is only payable on the value of your estate, calculated as above, which exceeds the tax threshold, the amount of your estate which is below the tax threshold being exempt.

Transferring any unused nil-rate band
Any unused inheritance tax nil-rate band of a married person that remains unused on death is transferable to a surviving spouse upon her subsequent death, no matter when the first person died and the same applies in the case of registered civil partners.

Transferability is limited to those who are legally married and to registered civil partners and is not available to others, e.g. to different sex partners who are not legally married or to same sex partners who have not registered a civil partnership or between parent and child or siblings and transferability is lost if the marriage or partnership is dissolved before the second death. Neither is transferability available on any other occasion but death; it is therefore not available when the survivor makes an immediately chargeable lifetime gift, but it is available against additional tax payable on the survivor's death in respect of the gift if the survivor dies within seven years of making the gift. Transferring any unused nil-rate band is discussed in greater detail on pages 128–134.

Any non-exempt gifts you make in the seven years prior to your death will reduce the tax threshold available to set against your estate at your death.

PETS and taper relief

Gifts (other than immediately chargeable gifts) made during your life are known as potentially exempt transfers (PETS) and, in the case of non-exempt gifts made between three and seven years before your death, only a proportion of the tax is charged, the proportion depending upon how long you survive the making of the gift.

◆ At the time of writing (2009) if you survive the making of the gift by over seven years no inheritance tax is payable in respect of the gift.

◆ If you survive the making of the gift by between six and seven years, tax is payable in respect of the gift at 20% of the death rate, i.e. at the rate of 8%.

◆ If you survive the making of the gift by between five and six years, tax is payable in respect of the gift at 40% of the death rate, i.e. at the rate of 16%.

◆ If you survive the making of the gift by between four and five years, tax is payable in respect of the gift at 60% of the death rate, i.e. at the rate of 24%.

◆ If you survive the making of the gift by between three and four years, tax is payable in respect of the gift at 80% of the death rate, i.e. at the rate of 32%.

This reduction of the tax payable on PETS is known as taper relief.

Benefiting from things you have given away

The reservation of a benefit rule
If, to use the technical term, you reserve a benefit from a gift, that
is to say retain an interest in or continue to benefit in some
significant way from the asset you give away without making
monetary payment at a commercial rate for the use or benefit, for
example, if you give away your house but

♦ continue to live in it at a less than a commercial rent; or
♦ retain the right to live in it as long as you wish prior to your
  death; or
♦ occupy it for the occasional holiday;

you will gain no inheritance tax relief in respect of the gift and it
will be counted as part of your estate when you die. Making a gift
to reduce inheritance tax must be a case of giving virtually
everything. You cannot have your cake and eat it. HM Revenue
and Customs takes a strict view of what constitutes reservation of
a benefit and considers that there is a reservation of a benefit if
the benefit is significant in relation to the value of the asset given.
To be a tax-effective gift, what is given must go almost in its
entirety and no real benefit can be retained, even by a behind-the-
scenes arrangement.

The rules relating to pre-owned assets
Various complicated schemes, (usually based upon the use of
trusts), have been marketed to avoid the inheritance tax liability
resulting from the gifts with a reservation of an interest rule. As
with any artificial arrangements which are solely for the purpose
of saving of tax you should think carefully before entering into

them because they have a habit of rebounding upon the taxpayer. In his budget in March 2004 the Chancellor of the Exchequer outlined proposals for a 'free standing income tax charge' based on 'pre-owned assets' to counteract such schemes and 'the benefit people get from having free or low cost enjoyment of assets they formerly owned or provided funds to purchase'. The proposals were enacted into law by Schedule 15 of the Finance Act 2004 and apply from 6 April 2005.

A 'note' was issued by the Treasury and what follows is largely based upon that note and the Act. To the extent that it is Crown copyright material, Crown copyright is acknowledged and it is reproduced with the general permission given by the Controller of HMSO.

The income tax charge is similar to the income tax charge made upon employees for benefits in kind supplied by their employers and quantifies in cash the annual benefit enjoyed. The charge applies both to tangible and intangible assets and to any funds or contributions to the funds used to acquire the assets whether the funds or contributions are directly or indirectly provided. It is equivalent in the case of property to the annual rental value of the asset or in the case of other assets, the value of the asset at a rate of interest, and in each case less any payment made under any legally binding agreement for the use of the asset.

After the deduction of the amount paid for the benefit, the sum so ascertained is added to your taxable income and taxed at your top rate of tax. The first £5,000 per annum is ignored but once the £5,000 exemption is exceeded, the exemption is totally lost and tax is payable on the entire sum, not just on the excess.

The income tax charge does not apply to the extent that:

- the asset was disposed of before 18 March 1986;

- the formerly owned asset is currently owned by your civil partner or your spouse;

- the asset still counts as an asset for inheritance tax purposes under the gift with a reservation rules;

- the asset was transferred to your spouse, former spouse, civil partner or former civil partner by court order;

- the asset was sold for cash at arm's length whether or not the parties were connected persons;

- the owner of the asset was formerly the owner of the asset only by virtue of a will or intestacy which has subsequently been varied by agreement between the parties (i.e. by a deed of family arrangement, as explained in Chapter 11);

- any enjoyment is no more than incidental, including cases where an out and out gift to a member of your family comes to benefit you as a result of a change in his circumstances;

- it is the case of an outright gift of money made more than seven years or more before the earliest date upon which you either occupied the land or had the use of the asset as applicable;

- the original gift was for the maintenance of your family or within the small gifts exemption (£250) or within the inheritance tax annual gifts allowance (£3,000);

- the asset given is land or buildings and the donor and the person to whom it is given share occupation of the land and either the donor pays all the running costs and capital expenses relating to the occupation of the property or an amount at least proportionate to his share of the ownership and use of the property so that he cannot be said to be retaining any benefit from the arrangement.

Former owners are not regarded as enjoying a taxable benefit if they retain an interest which is consistent with their ongoing enjoyment of the property. For example, the charge will not arise if your elderly mother who owns the whole of her home passes a 50% interest to you and you live with her. It could well apply if she gave a 90% interest to you.

If you so elect before 31 January after the end of the first tax year in which the pre-owned asset rules apply to you, you may choose to have the property concerned treated as part of your estate for inheritance tax purposes as a gift with reservation of an interest rather than have the benefit taxed as income. In those circumstances, the property would be eligible for the normal IHT reliefs and exemptions available, for example, to business and agricultural property reliefs. As to these reliefs, please see below. The election is made to the Capital Taxes Office on its specified form IHT 500 which is set out in the schedule to rather lengthily entitled statutory instrument number 3000 of 2007 'Income Tax (Benefits Received by Former Owners of Property Election for Treatment of Inheritance Tax) Regulations'.

If you have, or are deemed to have, a UK domicile, the scheme imposing the income tax liability in respect of pre-owned assets affects all your assets wherever the assets are; if you do not have and are not deemed to have a UK domicile, only your assets in the UK are affected.

If you give an asset away and pay a full commercial rent or hiring fee to use it, although doing so will save inheritance tax and a possible pre-owned assets charge, it will not be an otherwise tax efficient transaction because as far as income tax is concerned, you will be paying the rent out of your taxed income and the recipient of the gift will have to pay income tax on the rent. Moreover, if it was your principal private residence you will lose your capital gains tax exemption for a principal private residence.

Reliefs against inheritance tax

Taper relief has been covered on page 89. There are also certain circumstances and certain types of property viz. agricultural property, businesses (other than investment company or property businesses) and woodlands, which have been owned for at least two years prior to death, in respect of which relief is given against inheritance tax and it is either reduced or not charged at all.

Business property relief

How business property relief works

Business property relief operates to reduce by 100% or 50%, for inheritance tax purposes, the value of 'relevant business property' in a qualifying business which has been owned for two years and operates whether the property is situated here or overseas. Relevant business property that has been owned for less than two years but replaces relevant business property which has been owned for two of the preceding five years also qualifies for relief.

The amount of the reduction depends upon the type of relevant business property concerned.

What property is entitled to business relief?
Broadly speaking, relevant business property which is entitled to 100% relief consists of:

◆ your unincorporated business or share of an unincorporated business, such as your share in a partnership;

◆ your shares in a company which are not quoted on a recognised stock exchange (although most shares which are traded on the Alternative Investment Market (AIM) do benefit from 100% relief);

◆ securities that are not quoted on a recognised stock exchange, which you own and which, either by themselves or when combined with other unquoted shares or securities you own, give you control of the majority of the voting rights in the company;

◆ assets you use in the business that are assets of a trust of which you are a life tenant.

Relevant business property entitled to 50% relief consists of:

◆ securities or shares that you own in a company which are quoted on a recognised stock exchange and which, either by themselves or when combined with other quoted shares or securities you own, give you control of the majority of the voting rights in the company;

◆ assets that you own personally which are used, mainly or wholly by a qualifying business in which you are either a partner or a controlling shareholder.

It should be noted that directors' loans to a company are not, as such, entitled to business property relief and consideration should be given to the advisability and possibility of converting such loans into shares so that after two years their value will be entitled to relief. A partner's loan(s) to a partnership is entitled to business property relief because the money is credited to his partnership capital account and regarded as part of the partnership capital.

Business property relief does not apply to assets that have not been used wholly or mainly for the purpose of the business throughout the preceding two years or are not required for an identified future use in the business, e.g. investments of the business or excessive cash balances. Parts of buildings or land which are used exclusively for the business are treated separately and entitled to business relief if they fulfil the other requirements.

Assets of the business which have not been owned for the preceding two years can qualify if they replace assets that have been owned for two of the preceding five years. In the case of assets inherited from your spouse or registered civil partner, the period during which your spouse or civil partner owned the assets can be included to make up the period of two years of the two-year business property relief rule. Further, the two-year rule does not apply to otherwise qualifying relevant business property which was entitled to relief when it was acquired by you, by your spouse or civil partner, if either the current disposal or the earlier disposal was or is made on death.

What kind of businesses are entitled to business relief?
The business must be one that is carried on for profit and it must be

a trading business and not an investment business. The relief does not apply to businesses wholly or mainly engaged in dealing in land, buildings, securities, shares, or the making or holding of investments, although the business of a market maker or discount house in the United Kingdom qualifies for business relief. Neither does the relief apply to businesses or business property which are subject to a contract of sale at the relevant time, unless the sale is in return for shares in the acquiring company which will continue the business. Therefore the relief does not apply to a share in a partnership if it is a term of the partnership deed that the partnership share *must* be sold to the remaining partner or partners. However, if the share is the subject of a double option agreement, i.e. an agreement by which your surviving partner(s) are given an *option* to purchase your share on your death and your personal representatives are given an *option* to require them to purchase, then any sale is considered to take place post-death and will not prevent a claim for business property relief.

Agricultural property relief

How and when agricultural property relief is applied
In many ways agricultural property relief resembles business property relief. It operates to reduce for inheritance tax purposes the agricultural value transferred by a transfer of an asset by 100% or 50% and does not apply if the asset is under a binding contract for sale at the time of the disposition. The relief applies only to the agricultural value of the property concerned, i.e. it does not apply to the value which the property would have if it were used, or could ever be used, for any purpose other than agriculture. Consequently, the value of an asset for the purpose of calculating agricultural property relief is sometimes less than its

value as a business asset. If agricultural assets form part of a business, although double relief is not possible, it is sometimes possible to claim business relief on the excess of their business value over their value as agricultural assets if they do not qualify for agricultural property relief and if the appropriate conditions for business property relief are met. If assets qualify for both agricultural relief and business relief, only one relief is given and that relief is agricultural property relief.

Except for the situation set out in the next paragraph, to claim agricultural property relief you must either have occupied the property for agricultural purposes for the two years immediately preceding the disposition or it must have been owned by you throughout the period of seven years immediately preceding the disposition and occupied by you or by someone else for agricultural purposes throughout that period. If you inherited the property upon the death of your spouse or registered civil partner, the period of ownership and occupation by your spouse or civil partner can be included when computing the periods of occupation or ownership as the case may be and occupation by a company in which you control the majority of the voting rights counts as occupation by you.

If the property was entitled to agricultural relief when you, your spouse or your civil partner acquired it on a death or the present disposition occurs on your death, the relief can be claimed without the necessity for complying with the time conditions, provided that the property was occupied for agricultural purposes by the personal representatives of the person from whose estate it was acquired or you to occupy it when you die.

The property to which agricultural property relief applies

Agricultural property relief only applies to certain agricultural property situated in the United Kingdom, the Isle of Man or the Channel Islands and since 22 April 2009 to agricultural property in the European Economic Area. It does not apply to agricultural property situated elsewhere.

The agricultural property concerned is:

◆ agricultural land;

◆ woodlands and buildings occupied with agricultural land and used for the intensive rearing of livestock or fish if the occupation is ancillary to the use of the agricultural land. To be ancillary to the use of the agricultural land the woodland or buildings, as the case may be, must be used as a subordinate part of the farm;

◆ farmhouses and other farm buildings which are of a size and character appropriate to the requirements of the farm concerned and farm cottages occupied by agricultural employees of the farm. If the size of the 'farmhouse' is disproportionate to the size of the land being farmed with it and more like a country house, it will not be considered to be a farmhouse and not be entitled to agricultural property relief. The house must be ancillary to the farmland. The question to be decided is whether the holding is a farm or a house with land. Is it merely a place where the farmer of the farm lives, or in the words of one judge, 'a considerable residence'? Similarly if you own the 'farmhouse' and live in it but let the land to another who farms it, the 'farmhouse' will not be entitled to agricultural property relief because it will not be a farmhouse in the true sense of the word in that it is not occupied for the agricultural purpose of farming the land. The extent to which the person who occupies the farmhouse must be involved in the actual day-to-day working of the land to retain the farmhouse's entitlement to agricultural relief is an interesting but unresolved question. Is it sufficient that the occupier retains general control of the strategy and running of the farm and is entitled to its fluctuating profits whilst contracting out the day-to-day work on the farm to a manager, or must the occupier actually carry out the farming processes in person? Perhaps the best way of looking at the question is to ask how great a convenience or necessity it is for the occupier of the house to live there if he is to carry out the functions he carries out in connection with the farming of the land;

♦ growing crops transferred with the relevant land;

♦ stud farms for horses and associated pasture;

♦ land which is part of a habitat scheme;

♦ controlling shareholdings which meet the time test in farming companies that also meet the two- or seven-year test in relation to the qualifying assets of the companies, but only to the extent that the agricultural value of the companies' qualifying assets is represented in the shareholding. To calculate the proportion of the value of the shares in respect of which agricultural relief is available, divide the value of the company's eligible assets by the value of its total assets and multiply the resulting figure by the value of the shares. Agricultural property relief is not given in respect of shareholdings in such companies other than controlling shareholdings and is not given in respect of any value other than the agricultural value. It is not given in respect of directors' loans to agricultural limited companies as contrasted with their shareholdings. Nor is it given in respect of assets that are not eligible assets such as agricultural machinery or stock.

Which rate of relief applies?

The agricultural value of the asset transferred is reduced by 100% for inheritance tax purposes if:

♦ you have owner occupation or have the right to obtain vacant possession within 24 months; or

♦ you have an agricultural tenancy which commenced on or after 1 September 1995; or

♦ the case is the unusual one of land let on a tenancy commencing before 10 April 1981 in respect of which certain conditions apply and in respect of which transitional relief is given at 100%.

In all other cases it is reduced by 50%.

Agricultural relief and mortgaged property

If a mortgage is secured upon agricultural and non-agricultural property, it is necessary to apportion the amount of the mortgage between the agricultural value of the agricultural property and the full commercial value of the non-agricultural property in proportion to the respective values and then deduct the respective apportioned amounts of the mortgage from the respective gross values to ascertain the net value of each part. Agricultural relief at the appropriate rate is then applied to the net value agricultural value of the agricultural part and the resultant figure is then added to the

net value of the non-agricultural property to ascertain the total
value upon which inheritance tax is to be charged.

Agricultural and/or business property relief?
If assets qualify for both agricultural relief and business relief,
only one relief is given and that relief is agricultural property
relief. If farm assets do not qualify for agricultural property relief,
for example livestock or agricultural machinery, they might still
qualify for business property relief if the appropriate conditions
are met.

Woodland relief
In some circumstances you can obtain temporary relief from
inheritance tax on your death on the value of timber growing on
land (other than agricultural land) within the United Kingdom or
the European Economic Area. You cannot obtain relief on the
value of the land upon which the timber is growing. Throughout
the five years prior to your death you must have owned or had an
interest in possession (such as a life interest) in the land upon
which the timber is growing or you must have been given and not
purchased it. This condition is to prevent you from making a
deathbed purchase of woodland as a tax avoidance measure. The
relief is not available for disposals in your lifetime and must be
claimed by your personal representatives who must make an
election within two years of your death unless the Revenue is
prepared to exercise its discretion and accept an election made at
a later date.

Woodland relief does not apply to shares in companies which own
woodlands and is seldom used because the conditions for business
relief or agricultural relief can usually be complied with.

On a later disposal of the timber (other than to your widow or registered civil partner) inheritance tax is payable on its net value at the time of disposal but at the rate applicable on your death, unless the rate has been reduced when the appropriate rate is that applicable at the date of the disposal. The value of the timber is likely to be higher then than it was on your death. In calculating the net value, the expenses of replanting the woodland within three years and the expenses incurred in disposal can be deducted if they are not claimable for income tax.

Relief for heritage assets

Limited conditional relief is given in respect of land, buildings and objects which appear to the Treasury to be of outstanding importance from the point of view of the national heritage. The relief is dependent upon specified obligations designed to preserve the asset and afford public access to it in this country being undertaken by your beneficiaries.

Double taxation relief

If an asset which you own is situated in a foreign country with which the United Kingdom has a Double Taxation Agreement and it is subject to both United Kingdom inheritance tax and a tax similar to inheritance tax in the foreign country, relief will be given as a credit against the United Kingdom tax payable in respect of the overseas tax. The relief given is the lower of the foreign tax which will have to be paid in respect of the asset and the United Kingdom tax which would otherwise be payable in respect of the asset, the United Kingdom tax being calculated at the average percentage rate payable in respect of your estate.

The United Kingdom has Double Taxation Agreements with France, the Irish Republic, Italy, the Netherlands, South Africa,

Sweden and the United States of America. There is also an
agreement with Switzerland which applies to inheritance tax on
deaths but not on lifetime gifts or to tax on failed PETs.
Sometimes relief is also given unilaterally.

Other reliefs from inheritance tax exist but they cannot be planned
for and are consequently not material to a book on making a will.

INHERITANCE TAX ON TRUSTS SET UP IN YOUR WILL

Tax is charged upon your estate in the usual manner on your
death, allowing the usual exemptions, reliefs and for the nil charge
in respect of any unused nil-rate band. The following remarks
apply to inheritance tax during the life of the trusts.

Charitable trusts

Gifts for the purposes of charity as defined by the law are exempt
from inheritance tax if made in favour of a charity or charitable
trust established within the United Kingdom, whether they are
given during the taxpayer's lifetime or by his will. Inheritance tax is
not payable while trust assets are held exclusively for charitable
purposes, but if the trust deed provides that the trust assets are to
be held by the trustees for the charitable purpose for only a limited
period, an inheritance tax exit charge (albeit at a reduced rate
depending upon how long the trust fund has been held for
charitable purposes) will be payable when the assets cease to be
held for charitable purposes. There is no inheritance tax exit charge
levied when a discretionary trust makes a distribution to a charity.

Discretionary trusts

The trust funds of any non-charitable discretionary trusts created
by your will suffer an inheritance tax charge every ten years on

their value to the extent that they exceed the nil-rate band at that date. The current maximum rate is 6%. The tax is also charged upon any capital paid out of the trust at the same maximum rate, but if the trust is a nil-rate band trust there is no inheritance tax payable on capital paid out of the trust in the first ten years because in that period the tax rate is calculated upon the value of the trust at the date of the death which by definition did not exceed the nil-rate band. No tax is payable on the death of a potential beneficiary because the trust funds belong to the trust and do not belong to or form part of the estate of any potential beneficiary; no potential beneficiary has any entitlement until the trustees make an allocation to him.

With the exception of

- trusts for the disabled as defined in section 89 of the Inheritance Tax Act 1984;

- trusts for bereaved minors;

- 18–25 trusts;

- immediate post-death interest trusts;

- bare trusts;

- and charitable trusts;

interest in possession trusts are taxed for inheritance tax purposes in the same way as discretionary trusts.

Trusts for bereaved minors
These are trusts for the benefit of your under-age child who will become fully entitled to the trust funds at an age which is not

greater than 18. While the child is under the age of 18 any capital used for the benefit of a beneficiary must be used for his benefit and no income of the trust can be used for the benefit of any other person. The trust can be created by you if you are a parent, step-parent or other person who has parental responsibility for the child and must be created by your will or come into being on your intestacy. After any inheritance tax due on your death has been paid there is no further inheritance tax payable.

18–25 trusts

These are trusts which do not qualify as trusts for bereaved minors solely by reason of the fact that the beneficiary does not become entitled to the trust funds at the age of 18 or under. However, the beneficiary must become entitled to the trust funds at an age not greater than 25. While the beneficiary is under the age of 18 there is no liability for periodic ten-year anniversary charges and no exit charge upon payments being made to him. Payments to a beneficiary who is over the age of 18, or on the beneficiary's death between the age of 18 and 25, incur an exit charge which is calculated in the usual way from the date upon which the beneficiary became 18.

Immediate post-death interest trusts

Immediate post-death interest trusts are trusts created on death for a life tenant whose interest begins immediately on the death. These trusts are taxed as if the tenant for life is the owner of the trust funds. Consequently, unless the trust funds are excluded property, on the death of the life tenant the value of the trust fund is added to the value of his estate and inheritance tax is charged on the total sum, subject to the usual exceptions and reliefs. If the life tenant is your surviving spouse or civil partner the surviving spouse exemption applies. If the life tenant terminates his interest, e.g. by surrendering it, the termination is an immediately chargeable lifetime transfer if the trust continues, unless the continuing trust is a trust for charitable purposes or for the disabled or a bereaved minor's trust, in which cases the termination of the life interest operates as a PET by the life tenant. If the termination of the life interest puts an end to the trust the termination is a PET by the life tenant.

Bare trusts

A bare trust is a trust which exists when an asset is in the name of one or more people or organisations but is not to benefit them but is for the benefit of others – nothing more and nothing less, for example, 'to my executors upon trust for my son'. The beneficiary must be in existence when the trust comes into force and bare trusts cannot be created for the benefit of those who have not yet been conceived. Bare trusts are usually used to hold property when it would not be practical for legal or other reasons for the beneficiary to have the property in his own name, for example, if the beneficiary is under age or mentally incapable of managing it himself.

For inheritance tax purposes the beneficiaries of a bare trust are considered to own the trust fund. When an asset leaves the trust, because the asset is considered to be that of the beneficiary, there is no transfer of value for inheritance tax purposes if it is transferred out to the beneficiary. If it is transferred to some other person, e.g. on the beneficiary's death or upon his instructions during his lifetime, there will be a transfer of value to be taxed in accordance with the usual inheritance tax rules.

WHO BEARS THE INHERITANCE TAX?

In brief

◆ If you make a PET (including a transfer of value into a trust for disabled beneficiaries) no tax is payable unless you die within seven years in which case it is borne by the donee and taper relief will be available if you survive the gift by three years or more.

◆ If you make an immediately chargeable transfer (such as a transfer of value into a trust other than a trust for disabled beneficiaries or a transfer to a company) during your life and the transfer causes your unused nil-rate band to be exceeded

a) you can agree with the donee who will bear the immediately chargeable tax, but if you bear the tax the transfer will be treated as a gift of the sum given and of the relevant tax and the sum must be grossed up to ascertain the tax payable. The tax is payable at the lifetime rate which is one half of the rate chargeable on death;

b) if you die within seven years of making the gift additional tax will become payable to bring the tax paid up to the death rate and the additional tax will be the responsibility of and be borne by the donee irrespective of who paid the immediately chargeable lifetime rate tax.

◆ On your death the wording of your will can determine who pays any inheritance tax on bequests made by the will. Unless you state otherwise in your will, tax is borne by those who inherit your residuary estate except in the cases of:
  – jointly owned or foreign property, in which cases the tax is payable by the beneficiary; and

- residuary estates bequeathed between exempt beneficiaries (such as charities, your spouse or civil partner) and taxable beneficiaries, in which cases any inheritance tax which is payable on your estate must be paid out of the shares of your non-exempt beneficiaries after the estate has been divided between them and the exempt beneficiaries but before it is distributed.

◆ Any inheritance tax payable as the result of your death if you are entitled to a present interest in a trust for the disabled is borne by your personal representatives and the trustees of the trust in the proportion to the relative values of your own estate and the trust funds. To work out the proportions calculate an estate rate by dividing the total inheritance tax payable by the value of the total chargeable estate (your own assets and the trust funds in which you had an interest) and multiply the resulting figure by 100. The value of your own assets is then multiplied by the estate rate to ascertain the tax payable by your estate and the value of the trust funds is multiplied by the estate rate to ascertain the amount of the tax to be borne by the trust.

CALCULATING THE INHERITANCE TAX PAYABLE ON DEATH

To calculate the inheritance tax payable on a non-exempt lifetime gift, deduct the balance of the tax threshold which remains unused by previously made non-exempt gifts from the net value of the gift and apply the full tax rate to the resulting figure to obtain the figure for the tax. Then apply taper relief to the tax figure. Tax is only payable on lifetime chargeable gifts if the total of your chargeable gifts themselves exceed the tax threshold, in which case apply taper relief to the tax, not to the value of the gift.

To calculate the inheritance tax payable on your death estate, add the total of your net death estate to the total of your chargeable gifts and deduct any unused balance of the tax threshold. Apply the full tax rate to the resultant figure and then deduct the full tax payable on the lifetime gifts (calculated as above before the application of taper relief).

In both cases remember to apply business relief, agricultural relief and the relief for woodlands as explained above if they are relevant.

Who pays
the inheritance
tax. — does
executor pay it
out of the 'pot'
inheritance 'are'
before legacies is }
money
distributed?

Cup.l...

cleaners will be visiting

ne 2017

6

Reducing Your Inheritance Tax

REDUCING YOUR INHERITANCE TAX BY MAKING GIFTS IN YOUR LIFETIME

About giving

Inheritance tax calculations about giving are complex and if you have difficulty with them, don't worry too much, just remember that when once your estate crosses the inheritance tax exemption threshold, your beneficiaries will be paying tax at a very high rate on the excess and that any non-taxable gift you make, either in your lifetime or by your will, will only cost your estate £60 for every £100 given because the other £40 would have been payable to the Revenue as inheritance tax. It is therefore important to make the best use possible of any inheritance tax exemptions and from a tax point of view, provided you do not impoverish yourself, it is an excellent idea to give as much as you can away in your lifetime and the sooner you give it, the more tax you will save. Non-taxable gifts of income producing assets reduce both your inheritance and income tax liabilities and, if made at the appropriate time and judiciously chosen, can also reduce future capital gains tax liability. Moreover, immediately taxable gifts made in your lifetime suffer inheritance tax at only one half of the tax rate suffered by taxable gifts occurring on death and gifts made during your lifetime which were not then immediately chargeable might escape tax altogether as PETS, or if they become taxable on your death might be taxable at a lower rate by reason of taper relief. You might also have the pleasure of seeing the recipients enjoy the gifts and perhaps even make good use of them, something that it is debatable that you will be able to do after your death!

In deciding whether what you give away in your lifetime will impoverish you, do not forget the effect of inflation and remember that you cannot have your cake and eat it. To be a tax-effective gift it must go virtually completely and you cannot retain any significant benefit from it, even by a behind-the-scenes arrangement.

Remember that both parties to a marriage or to a registered civil partnership have their own set of gift exemptions and that asset transfers to a spouse or registered civil partner are exempt from capital gains tax and stamp duty. Sharing assets with, or giving assets to, your spouse or registered civil partner if she owns less than the inheritance tax threshold might enable her to make tax-free gifts to others which she might otherwise be unable to make and in this way use her otherwise unusable exemptions and at the same reduce your own potential tax liabilities. Any transfer of assets or cash to enable your spouse/civil partner to make use of gift exemptions must not be made *conditional* upon such further gifts being made or it will be caught by the rule against associated operations and not reduce your tax.

Deciding what to give and to whom

When deciding which assets to give, consider giving the assets with the greatest growth potential because the asset given will be valued as at the date you make the gift and the gift of assets with the greatest growth between the date of the gift and the date of your death will bring about the greatest reduction in the value of your estate for inheritance tax purposes, if you survive the seven years.

If you are able to make such gifts to younger rather than older individuals, so much the better because in the normal course of things they will have longer to live before inheritance tax is payable on the recipients' deaths. Some think that you should bear in mind and tend to retain assets which might receive some inheritance tax relief or exemption such as gifts of shares in unquoted companies which have been held for two years or more, some business property and agricultural property and commercial woodlands. Others believe that the relief given to these assets are over generous and might therefore be reduced or abolished in the future. If possible give assets that can benefit from inheritance tax relief to those who are qualified and able to use them so that the reliefs are not wasted.

In the choice of which assets should be given and which retained, bear in mind which assets are exempt from capital gains tax and that there is no capital gains payable on death, so that assets on which you already have a large capital gain might be those to retain unless they can be given away under your annual capital gains exemption limit.

Gifts of the family home, or a share in the home, deserve a special mention because there are both financial and emotional factors involved. If you are contemplating such a gift you should seek independent and expert advice. My advice is that you should keep a roof over your head and retain your independence and security by retaining ownership of the family home as long as you can rather than having to rely upon the goodwill of the family. It is not worth risking homelessness for the sake of reducing tax. Too often a child whose business is in financial difficulties has decided that it would be better for an elderly parent to pass the family home to him to avoid inheritance tax on the parent's death or future home fees and incidentally allow him to use it as collateral security for a loan to support the failing business.

The financial services industry has dreamt up ingenious and complex schemes to permit you to continue to occupy your home as long as you wish but at the same time reduce or eliminate its value for inheritance tax purposes on your death. Such schemes are fraught with potential problems and if you enter into them you should do so in the full knowledge that they may well not succeed and if they do not do so it is your estate and not the financial service provider that will bear the loss. You have only to remember the introduction of the pre-owned assets charge which was brought in to counter artificial transactions solely entered into for the purpose of reducing tax and took effect retrospectively to upset transactions that had been effected, sometimes 19 years earlier, to realise that if such schemes do succeed they can be overturned by any government.

Any scheme to reduce inheritance tax involving a change of ownership of the family home which fails can result in disastrous consequences all round: in many cases there will be no saving of inheritance tax or an income tax liability under the pre-owned assets charge will arise and unless the recipients of the home occupy it as their principal private residence, any gain that they make when they dispose of the property will be taken into account when assessing their liability to capital gains tax.

In addition to fiscal risks of a scheme involving loss of ownership of the family home failing there can be other dangers and problems. Suppose, for example, you decide to give or sell a share of the family home to your daughter. After the gift your daughter and you will both own and be entitled to use the house. This might not be a good idea, especially if your daughter:

♦ gives her share of the house away in your joint lifetimes; or

♦ marries; or

♦ predeceases you married, but intestate, or with a will which leaves her estate to her husband/partner who remarries, or to any third party; or

♦ becomes bankrupt.

Apart from any question of problems that might arise from sharing the use of the home, the new part-owner might wish to cash in the share of the house and attempt to force a sale. While you might justifiably think you can rely upon your daughter not attempting to force a sale, can you rely upon her future husband who you might not even have met at the time of your gift or upon her or his trustee in bankruptcy?

What will happen if after making the gift you decide that you wish to move elsewhere? Would this necessitate a sale of the property, perhaps against your co-owner's wishes? Will your share of the net proceeds of the sale and any other funds you have be sufficient for you to acquire another property?

A lifetime gift of a share of the family home to a child who lives with you can create particular problems if you have several children, all of whom you wish to benefit equally and you intend to compensate the others by bequests in your will. When considering the provision to be made in the will, account will have to be taken of the fact that neither the size of the estate at the unpredictable date of your death nor the variation in the value of the share in the house between the date of the gift and that date can be calculated in advance with any certainty.

When choosing beneficiaries also bear in mind the effect on any social security benefits they are receiving.

Lifetime gifts by terminally ill spouses and civil partners

If one spouse or partner becomes terminally ill, try to make use of exempt lifetime gifts to the maximum as each tax year progresses and use the fact that lifetime gifts between spouses or registered civil partners are exempt from both inheritance and capital gains taxes to ensure that any estate of the spouse or partner who is likely to die first which is not to be left to the survivor will exceed the exempt threshold by as little as possible; the survivor can then use his own lifetime gift exemptions to make gifts from the excess to the intended beneficiaries which would have been taxable if made on the first death.

Keeping records

The percentage of the value of any gift which is not an exempt disposition or a gift of excluded property that is extracted as tax, i.e. the actual rate of tax charged, is dependant upon:

◆ whether the gift is deemed to have been made at the time of your death or whether it was made during your life and if so how long you survive the making of the gift;

◆ who or what organisation was the recipient of the gift; and

◆ the type of property given,

It is therefore essential to keep full documentary evi
shows the dates and the value of all gifts, what was g~~~ ~~
whom the gifts were made. If it is likely that the normal
expenditure exemption will be relied upon it is also necessary to
keep details of all income, income tax paid, spending, bills and
other expenses for the relevant year at least.

REDUCING INHERITANCE TAX BY MAKING A WILL

Using exempt gifts in your will

Several of the types of gift which are exempt from inheritance tax
if made during your lifetime are also exempt if made by your will,
notably:

- gifts to registered charities for their charitable purposes;

- the gifts for national purposes including gifts to most museums
  and art galleries;

- gifts to some political parties;

- gifts of land to housing associations;

- gifts to your spouse or civil partner;

- gifts the value of which does not exceed your unused nil-rate
  band.

Making any of these gifts in your will reduces the inheritance tax
which would otherwise be payable.

Equalisation of estates between spouses and between civil partners

The pre-2008 Finance Act position

If, before the Finance Act 2008, you were in a happy marriage or civil partnership and believed that you were likely to remain so, then because there was no means of knowing which spouse or partner would be the first to die, the most obvious and effective way of reducing the amount of inheritance tax payable on your death and the death of your partner or your spouse was to equalise your taxable estates during your joint lives by the richer making gifts to the other and for each of you to make full use of the survivor exemption and the nil-rate band. You did this by leaving value up to the nil-rate band to beneficiaries other than your spouse or partner and the remainder of your estate to your spouse or partner. Whether or not you could afford to do so depended upon the total value of your joint estates, the state of your marriage or civil partnership and the standard of living each of you were accustomed to and were prepared to accept.

However, in considering how to equalise the estates and whether or not it was be sensible to equalise the estates, as always, it was necessary to bear in mind the effect on your income tax positions. From an income tax point of view, it was best, as far as possible, to ensure that both parties made equal use of their lower and basic rate income tax bands and this might decide which party should hold which assets and, indeed, whether and to what extent you should have equalised your assets to help with inheritance tax planning.

After the Finance Act 2008

Since the coming into force of the Finance Act 2008 and the introduction of the transferability of the nil-rate band, equalisation of estates between spouses has been considered by many to be unnecessary and has become a much less common procedure but it might still prove to be a wise precaution if a future government were to decide to institute a wealth tax. In some cases it also puts the recipient in a better position to make lifetime gifts and use the lifetime gift exemptions.

Nil-rate band discretionary trusts

Although you could leave your entire estate to your spouse or registered civil partner without paying any inheritance tax on your death, before the Finance Act 2008 Act was passed, doing so might have compounded the inheritance tax problem when your spouse or partner subsequently died, in that what you left and she did not give away seven years or more before her death or spend before her death, would be added to the assets she already held in her name and in many cases to the assets of a trust under which she had a right to benefit during her lifetime and might thus have caused her estate to exceed the nil-rate band and incur 40% tax.

On the other hand, if you were only moderately well off, your surviving spouse or civil partner would need the family home and your other assets to live reasonably comfortably after your death and assets could not easily be given to others to make use of your nil-rate band. This dichotomy could be solved to some extent by making use of a nil-rate band discretionary trust of which your spouse or civil partner was one of the potential beneficiaries and leaving the remainder of your estate to your spouse or partner (as described later in this chapter).

Since the Finance Act 2008 equalisation of estates and the use of the nil-rate band discretionary will trusts have, in most cases,

fallen out of use and been replaced by claiming transferability of
the nil-rate band. However, for some time yet many will continue
to exist and in some circumstances and for reasons other than
inheritance tax, they will continue to have some uses. For these
reasons a discussion of them is included in this book.

WARNING
No one should contemplate setting up or managing a trust without assistance from a lawyer who has considerable expertise in trusts and taxation. Trusts and the taxation of trusts are very technical subjects and the law and practice of trusts and taxation are in a state of constant evolution.

The basics of a nil-rate band discretionary will trust scheme are
that a discretionary trust is set up in the will of a married person
or a civil partner to the value of the testator's unused nil-rate
band and the testator's other assets are left to the testator's
spouse or civil partner. On the testator's death the assets left to
the trust are exempt from inheritance tax because they do not
exceed the testator's nil-rate band and the remainder of the estate
escapes inheritance tax under the surviving civil partner/spouse
exemption. The potential beneficiaries of the trust include the
survivor who is frequently appointed to be one of the trustees of
the trust. The intention is that the surviving spouse/civil partner
shall benefit from the trust funds or the income they produce from
time to time during her lifetime, as far as is considered necessary
or desirable. It is therefore possible that the survivor will have the
benefit of the entirety of the testator's estate and be in no worse a
position than she would have been if the assets had been left to
her directly but there is, and necessarily should be, no guarantee,
because it is the essence of a discretionary trust that the allocation
of the trust funds and their income shall be in the discretion of

the trustees and no one shall have a *right* to benefit from them unless the trustees make a decision to that effect.

If the first spouse/partner to die leaves sufficient liquid assets, such as cash or investments, they are transferred to the trustees of the trust and then the trustees are able to exercise their discretion to make such payments to the survivor as the trustees think fit. There is no problem, the survivor has the security of ownership of the entirety of the family home, there is a reduction in the inheritance tax that would have been payable on the second death and the survivor has the possibility (but not a guarantee because it involves the exercise by the trustees of their discretion in her favour) of benefiting from the estate to the extent that she would have benefited from it if it had been left directly to her.

Using the family home in a nil-rate band legacy discretionary will trust scheme
If the first spouse/partner to die leaves insufficient liquid assets, such as cash or investments, to use to pay the nil-rate band legacy and the survivor wishes to continue to live in the family home, the survivor and the trustees of the discretionary trust resort to using either the debt/charge or the loan discretionary trust scheme referred to in the following sections of this chapter.

If the family home is jointly owned and it is intended to use the testator's share of the home in a discretionary trust scheme, the co-owners must own the home as tenants in common and not as joint tenants because property owned as joint tenants passes on death to the survivor notwithstanding any provisions to the contrary in the deceased's will. If the home is owned as joint tenants the co-ownership joint tenancy must first be severed and converted into a tenancy in common.

Severance of a beneficial joint tenancy is a simple transaction that
must be carried out before your death and not by your will, but it
can be easily and cheaply carried out as explained below without
the assistance of a solicitor.

How do you know whether jointly-owned property is held as joint
tenants or tenants in common? As a first step the wording of the
title documents should be considered. Married couples and civil
partners usually, but not necessarily, own their homes as joint
tenants. If there is any evidence to show that joint owners own
separate shares of the property as opposed to each joint owner
owning the entirety, the joint ownership is a case of tenancies in
common. Joint tenants always own property equally and words or
actions indicating that the joint owners own unequally always
means that the assets are held as tenants in common.

Conversion of a joint tenancy into a tenancy in common by
severing it can be achieved by one joint tenant merely writing and
signing a note to the other(s) informing the other(s) that the joint
tenant is severing the joint tenancy by the note. ('I give you notice
that I hereby sever the joint tenancy which exists between us in the
property known as...') will suffice. The note should be handed to
the other co-owner(s) and it is a wise precaution to arrange for
the other co-owner(s) to sign a receipt (which can be written on a
copy of the note) to confirm that they have received the document
and to place the receipted copy of the document with the title
documents. If the property has a title which is registered at HM
Land Registry, the receipted copy should be sent to the Land
Registry at the District Land Registry, (the address of which can
be find noted on the official copy of the Land Registry title

information document) for noting in the Registry's records. When communicating with the Land Registry always quote the Land Registry Title Number which appears in the copy of the title information document.

It is possible for a joint tenant to sever the joint tenancy and create a tenancy in common by other conduct showing an intention to do so, but such a severance is much more difficult to prove.

The debt/charge discretionary will trust scheme

This is a scheme that is often used if the first spouse/partner to die leaves insufficient liquid assets (such as cash or investments) to use to pay the nil-rate band legacy, the survivor wishes to continue to live in the family home and the trustees do not wish to risk a large capital gains tax bill on the first to die's share of the family home when it is eventually sold.

The will setting up the trust will have contained a clause which authorises the trustees of the trust to accept an unsecured debt repayable on demand or a charge on assets as part or as the entirety of the trust funds. If the first spouse/partner to die leaves insufficient liquid assets to be transferred to the trust to fulfil the legacy, the trustees exercise that power and the deceased's executors give the trustees an IOU for the nil-rate band legacy or the deficiency or place a charge in favour of the trust upon assets of the estate and then transfer the assets including the deceased testator's share of the family home to the survivor subject to the charge. Placing a charge on the assets is, in layman's terms, mortgaging them to the trust.

The debt or charge is paid off when the assets are sold or as and when the survivor is able to repay it or when the survivor dies. If it still exists at the survivor's death the debt or charge will reduce the value of the survivor's estate and consequently any inheritance tax payable in respect of the estate.

The Loan Scheme

A variant of the debt/charge scheme is the Loan Scheme under which assets are loaned by the trust to the survivor who signs an IOU for them. The effect of Section 103 of the Finance Act 1986 is that a person cannot give cash or assets to another and then borrow them back and count the debt or borrowing as a debt against the estate for inheritance tax purposes. Section 103 therefore prevents the Loan Scheme from successfully reducing the tax if the spouse/ partner who dies is one who has never had assets not derived from the survivor spouse/partner, e.g. a spouse who has never worked and never had an inheritance. The Loan Scheme seems to differ little from the Debt/Charge Scheme but in the Debt/Charge Scheme it is the executors and not the survivor who create the charge or sign the IOU. The Loan Scheme is much riskier and more likely to be considered by the Revenue to be an artificial scheme entered into solely for the purpose of avoiding tax and a sham.

Warnings

- I repeat that anyone contemplating a discretionary trust must employ an expert. Remember that as is the case with most tax avoidance schemes – they are comlex, expensive if they go wrong and they are often difficult or impossible to unscramble if the law changes. If a government feels that too much tax is being lost it might decide to clamp down on the trusts and even introduce retrospective legislation to do so

- A nil-rate band discretionary trust will only be effective in reducing inheritance tax if it can be seen to be a genuine discretionary trust and not a sham simply aimed at avoiding tax. The trustees should therefore hold regular meetings, minutes should be taken and kept, the trust's investments should be monitored, accounts kept, income tax returns made and the needs of each potential beneficiary should be considered and resolutions passed. Not all the income of the trust should be paid to the survivor and it certainly should not be paid by regular payments or a bank mandate. A near cash reserve should be maintained to meet tax and administrative expenses and if necessary part of the loan should be recalled to meet them. The debt or loan can be structured to be index linked or bear interest. Every effort should be made to show that the trust is not merely a gift to the survivor in which case it would form part of the survivor's estate and be taxable when he or she died.

- Nil-rate band discretionary will trust legacy schemes only work if there is a valid marriage or registered civil partnership; there is no such thing in English law as a 'common law wife' or a 'common law husband' and the survivor exemption from inheritance tax does not apply in the cases of different sex partners who are not legally married or same sex partners who have not registered their partnership.

- If there is a danger that your net estate will be insufficient to meet the nil-rate band legacy to the trust and leave sufficient value for the home to be transferred to your spouse/civil partner, you will need to consider carefully what you intend to achieve and the wording of your will. If you leave a specific legacy of your unused nil-rate band to the trust and your home

is included in the residue of your estate the legacy will fall to be
paid in full and residuary estate (including the home) will be
reduced to meet the shortfall. If your spouse/civil partner wishes
to have the home transferred to her it will be necessary to make
arrangements to meet the legacy. In the same circumstances of
an insufficiency, if your home is bequeathed to your spouse/civil
partner subject to the legacy, the legacy will be reduced as far as
is necessary and your home will be unaffected.

Taxation of nil-rate band discretionary will trusts
Tax is charged on the estate of the person whose will sets up the
trust, at his death, in the usual manner allowing for the nil charge
for any unused nil-rate band. As is usual with discretionary
trusts, the trust funds might suffer an inheritance tax charge every
ten years if they exceed the nil-rate band at that date. The current
maximum rate for the charge is 6%. The tax is also charged upon
capital paid out of the trust at the same maximum rate but there
is no inheritance tax payable on capital paid out of the trust in
the first ten years because in that period the tax rate is calculated
upon the value of the trust at the date of the death which by
definition did not exceed the nil-rate band. Neither is tax payable
on the death of a potential beneficiary because the trust funds
belong to the trust and do not belong to or form part of the
estate of any potential beneficiary. No potential beneficiary has
any entitlement until the trustees make an allocation to him.

Using nil-rate band legacies without a discretionary trust
If you are married or in a civil partnership you can save
inheritance tax by each making use of your respective nil-rate
band by leaving a legacy equivalent to the value of the unused nil-
rate band to others and the residue of the estate to your surviving

spouse/partner or a charity without the necessity of a discretionary trust if you wish, but by not using a nil-rate band discretionary trust you lose the flexibility which a discretionary trust gives and the surviving spouse/civil partner will not have the possibility of benefiting from the funds bequeathed by the legacy.

Similarly if you have no civil partner or spouse and you leave the residue of your estate for charitable purposes and a legacy equivalent to the balance of your unused nil-rate band to others your estate will suffer no inheritance tax.

The advantages of using a nil-rate band discretionary will trust
The main advantage of using a discretionary trust, instead of a straight legacy, is flexibility. The trustees' powers can be used to meet differing circumstances which arise from time to time and circumstances which could not be foreseen at the time the trust was created. Your spouse/civil partner can be appointed as a trustee if your will so provides and your trustees can make income and capital payments in her favour as appropriate having regard to her needs, the size of the residue she inherits, her tax position and any social security benefits and entitlements. She need be little worse off than if the entire estate had been left to her and the funds formed part of her estate and were potentially taxable on her death. At the same time the trustees are able to consider and meet the needs of the other potential beneficiaries. Because the trust is discretionary and the funds belong to the trust and not to the survivor they will not be taken into account for means-tested benefits.

The cost of setting up and administering a discretionary trust are substantial but have to be compared with the tax saving which can be achieved. The transferable nil-rate band introduced by the Finance Act 2008 will result in fewer nil-rate band discretionary trusts being used.

The transferable nil-rate band

Transferring any unused nil-rate band
Any of the inheritance tax nil-rate band of a married person that remains unused on his death is transferable to his surviving spouse and can be used upon her subsequent death, no matter when he died and the same applies in the case of registered civil partners.

Transferability is limited to those who are legally married (including those who entered into a marriage abroad which is recognised here) and to registered civil partners. It is not available to others, e.g. to different sex partners who are not legally married or to same sex partners who have not registered a civil partnership or between parent and child. HMRC has stated that for the purpose of transferability of the unused nil-rate band, if a polygamous marriage ceremony entered into abroad is recognised as legal in the country where it took place all parties will be treated as 'spouses' for the purpose of transferability of the nil-rate band. As far as I am aware it has not expressed any view on polyandrous unions.

Transferability is lost if the marriage or partnership is dissolved before the second death. Neither is transferability available on any other occasion but death; it is therefore not available when the survivor makes an immediately chargeable lifetime gift, but it is available against additional tax payable on the survivor's death in respect of the gift if the survivor dies within seven years of making the gift.

If you have had more than one previous marriage or civil partnership that ended in death, the unused nil-rate bands of all of your previous spouses or partners can be transferred up to a maximum transferable amount equal to 100% of the nil-rate band at the date of your death. The unused nil-rate band available on your death is increased by the proportion of the nil-rate band that remained unused immediately after the previous death of your spouse/civil partner, for example, if the earlier death took place in June 2002 and involved a taxable estate of £125,000 when the nil-rate band was £250,000, 50% of the nil-rate band was unused on the first death and if your death takes place in December 2009, when the nil-rate band is £325,000, it will be possible for your personal representatives to claim an increase of 50% of the 2009/10 nil-rate band on the your death to increase the 2009/2010 death nil-rate band from £325,000 to £487,500. It is the mathematical proportion of the unused nil-rate band which is transferable, not the unused cash sum. For this reason nil-rate band trusts can in certain circumstances be counterproductive; the beneficiary of the nil-rate band benefits at a time when the nil-rate band is lower than at the date of the survivor's death.

If the entire estate is left to a surviving spouse or a civil partner under an arrangement effected by a tax compliant two-year discretionary trust as explained later or presumably under a tax compliant deed of family arrangement, none of the previously unused nil-rate band will be used and 100% will be transferable.

Inheritance tax replaced capital transfer tax which had itself replaced estate duty. Any unused allowances of a predeceasing spouse who died under the rules relating to capital transfer tax or estate duty may be used to increase the nil-rate band of the surviving spouse. In respect of deaths before 21 March 1972, when for the first time under the estate duty system a £15,000 surviving spouse exemption was introduced, these allowances will not include a surviving spouse exemption and will be based on the basic individual allowances. In respect of deaths under the capital transfer system which was introduced on 13 March 1975, the surviving spouse and nil-rate band provisions apply in the same way as they apply for inheritance tax.

The law did not provide for registered civil partnerships before 5 December 2005 and consequently there was no surviving civil partner's allowance before that date.

The claim to transfer must be made on the prescribed Inland Revenue form IHT 216 which is downloadable from HM Revenue and Customs' website and it must be made within 24 months of the month in which the last death took place. The claim must be supported by factual information and documentation concerning the earlier death. Probate or letters of administration of the first to die must be supplied, together with a copy of the death and marriage or civil partnership registration certificates, any will and any deeds of variation of the will. The amount of the nil-rate band available for transfer will not be agreed on the first death. It is therefore wise to retain the entire probate files relating to your predeceasing spouse/civil partner until you die and for those who will be your personal representatives to be made aware of where the relevant documents are kept.

The effect of the introduction of the transferable nil-rate band
Since the introduction of the transferable nil-rate band there are
fewer estates liable to inheritance tax and schemes using nil-rate
band discretionary trusts or equalisation of estates between
spouses and between civil partners to reduce inheritance tax are
used less frequently because it is possible to achieve the same
inheritance tax results by claiming transferability of the unused
nil-rate band. However, equalisation of estates will continue to be
useful to minimise the assets that will be available for assessment
when calculating nursing or residential home fees and if there is a
real fear of a future government imposing a wealth tax.

Choosing from the available post-9 October 2007 routes
After the Finance Act 2008 there are three possible routes from
which you can choose:

♦ use a nil-rate band discretionary trust; or

♦ leave a legacy or assets equivalent in value to your unused nil-
rate band directly to the beneficiary (in which case your
surviving spouse or civil partner will not be able to benefit
from it); or

♦ transfer the assets to your spouse/civil partner so that that the
unused nil-rate band can be used on her death.

Nil-rate-band discretionary trusts might still be useful, if made
during your life:

♦ to minimise the assets that will be available when calculating
nursing or residential home fees; or

♦ if there is a real fear of a future government imposing a wealth
tax.

They will still be useful in your will if you are undecided and wish to retain some flexibility and have a second bite at the asset allocation cake through your trustees. In appropriate circumstances thc trustees can still give your surviving spouse/civil partner the benefit of the nil-rate band by exercising their discretion and making an outright transfer of assets to her and the unused nil-rate band will then be available on her subsequent death.

You might choose to make a gift of the value of the nil-rate band directly to the beneficiary rather than allow your surviving spouse's or civil partner's estate to benefit from it or to create a discretionary trust if:

◆ you wish to have certainty, for example, if you are in a second marriage and wish to have the certainty that the children of your first marriage shall benefit; or

◆ you can give the legacy in assets which you believes will increase in value quicker than future increases in nil-rate bands.

You might choose to transfer the assets to your surviving spouse or civil partner so that the unused nil-rate band can be used on her death because:

◆ to do so will enable your spouse or partner to have the use of the assets without the expense and labour involved in running a discretionary trust;

◆ the traditional increases in the nil-rate band mean that the unused nil-rate band is likely to be worth more in cash terms at the time of her death than at the date of your death. This will happen because the transferable amount is the same proportion of the nil-rate band on the second death as the unused nil-rate band on the first death bears to the full nil-rate band at the time of the first death. To put the point another way if, for example, 40% of the nil-rate band applicable at the date of the first death is unused, that figure in cash terms is less than 40% of the increased nil-rate band applicable at the time of the second death.

If you really wish your spouse to benefit from the entirety of your estate but you used a nil-rate band will trust purely to save inheritance tax and in the hope that the trustees will use the trust to benefit your spouse or civil partner after your death but during her life or if you have left an outright nil-rate band legacy in favour of others for the same reason, you should now revise the will to leave your assets directly to your spouse or partner. To do so will mean that she will have the certainty of inheriting without, in the one case, the necessity of relying upon the trustees discretion and in the other case, relying upon a deed of family arrangement to which the alternative beneficiaries might not agree.

Even after the 2008 Finance Act it is still worth making lifetime gifts in appropriate circumstances because if they qualify as PETS you might survive long enough for them to drop out of the remaining nil-rate band calculation or to benefit from some taper relief. If they are immediately chargeable gifts they will suffer tax at only 50% of the death rate they will suffer if the nil-rate band is exceeded. Similarly if you have a spouse or civil partner but wish to make gifts to other family members or to friends then, depending upon your ethical standards, you might wish to consider an informal arrangement whereby you leave a larger part of your estate to your spouse/civil partner on an informal, unenforceable and undocumented agreement that the survivor will make gifts to the family or friends after your death and survive long enough for the tax benefits to be obtained.

On a mercenary note, from a purely financial point of view, it will sometimes pay a surviving spouse/civil partner to stay single. Consider, for example, the case of a widow who has a 100% transferable nil-rate band from her deceased husband in addition to her 100% nil-rate band and a widower who also has a 100% transferable nil-rate band from his previous marriage. Between them they have the equivalent of four nil-rate bands. If they marry, because the maximum total of unused nil-rate bands of all previous spouses or partners that can be transferred is equal to 100% of the nil-rate band at the date of a second death, they will only have two.

Using a two-year discretionary will trust

Because you cannot foretell the precise date of your death, you cannot know what the financial position of the individual members of your family will be at that date or indeed which of your family members or friends will survive you. Neither can you know how much of your nil-rate band will have been used up by the gifts you have made in your lifetime nor what the value of your estate or tax rates will be when you die. It is possible to overcome these problems by creating what is commonly known as a two-year discretionary trust in your will.

To create such a trust you leave your estate to your executors upon trust, with power for them to allocate it between three months and two years of your death, in such a manner as they see fit between certain specified beneficiaries and with a long stop provision for the devolution of the estate if your executors fail to make an allocation within that period. It is usual to leave a letter with your will to explain to your executors the principles you wish them to use in exercising the discretion you have given to them. The letter should make it clear that it is not binding upon your executors.

If the executors make their decision between three months and two years following your death, inheritance tax in relation to your estate will be calculated as though the decision they make was contained in your will.

A two-year discretionary trust can be a very efficient tax-saving tool and useful if you have good executors and are apt to be tardy in reviewing your will. It should not be confused with a nil-rate band discretionary trust.

Using the inheritance tax reliefs

It is a waste of an inheritance tax relief such as business property relief or agricultural property relief if you leave an asset that attracts the relief to exempt beneficiaries such as your spouse or civil partner, unless she intends to give or bequeath the asset to a non-exempt beneficiary in the future. It is better to specifically bequeath the asset to chargeable people or create a discretionary trust of which chargeable people are potential beneficiaries by your will and place the asset into the trust so that the relief is used. If the asset is eligible for 100% relief the bequest can be made without adverse inheritance tax consequences and will not use up any part of your unused nil-rate band.

It is also usually better that you leave relievable assets to those able to qualify for the relief in the future and should they not be chargeable persons, you can leave the assets to the chargeable beneficiaries so that the estate is relieved and the exempt person can possibly be left a compensating legacy or share of residue to enable her to purchase the asset from the original beneficiary. If you have insufficient assets to leave the legacy or share of residue bearing in mind the number of legatees you wish to include in your will and the size of the intended bequests, the purchase could perhaps be funded by taking out life policies during and on your life, underwritten on trust for the proposed purchaser, the premiums for which are paid using exempt gifts such as the small gifts or the annual exemptions. The proceeds of the policies will be outside your estate and your estate will be reduced by the amount of the premiums paid.

Leaving businesses or shares in companies that are entitled to business or agricultural property relief to those who can benefit from the reliefs and who are family members will help to keep control of the business or company within your family.

You should bequeath the assets as specific gifts and not included them in a share of residue. If you specifically bequeath an asset it will have the full benefit of the relief; if you bequeath it as part of the residue of your estate the relief will be apportioned between all the assets of the residuary estate including residue or shares of residue bequeathed to exempt beneficiaries. If an asset is appropriated by your personal representatives in satisfaction of a share of residue or a cash legacy, it will not be considered to have been specifically bequeathed and the bequest will not attract the

full relief, only its apportioned proportion. If your spou:
partner wishes to have the relievable asset you can consid
leaving it to chargeable beneficiaries (so that your estate will
benefit from the relief) but on terms that your spouse/civil partner
shall have an option to purchase it. Stamp Duty Land Tax and
Land Registry Fees might be payable on the purchase but they are
likely to be much less than the inheritance tax saved.

Calculating the nil-rate band special rules where exempt beneficiaries are involved

'Grossing-up' of legacies and gifts

Reference has previously been made to the grossing-up of
immediately chargeable lifetime gifts. If you do not state that any
tax payable in respect of a bequest in your will is to be paid out of
the bequest, i.e. that the bequest is subject to tax or to bear its
own tax, then unless the property is jointly owned or foreign
property, any tax payable will be payable out of the residue of
your estate. In these circumstances, if you leave the residue of your
estate to an exempt beneficiary such as your spouse or a registered
charity, the law directs that, when calculating the inheritance tax
payable in respect of your estate, for inheritance tax purposes, any
legacies given free of tax shall be 'grossed up' i.e. treated as a
legacy of the stated sum and in addition the relevant amount of
tax. If you do not remember this point, i.e. that any non-exempt
legacy given free of tax is grossed up if the residue of the estate is
given to an exempt beneficiary, you could inadvertently exceed the
nil-rate band with the legacy. You should also bear in mind any
non-exempt lifetime gifts you have made when calculating what
remains to you of the nil-rate band.

HM Revenue and Customs publish grossing-up tables to help you calculate the sums involved, but the easiest way of avoiding trouble in these circumstances is to give the bequests 'subject to tax' and not 'free of tax', or to leave legacies of specific amounts to the exempt beneficiaries and the residue to the non-exempt beneficiaries, to be inherited by them in specified proportions or percentages with a provision that should a residuary beneficiary not be alive or in existence at the date of your death, that beneficiary's interest in your residuary estate shall not lapse but shall accrue to the remaining beneficiaries in the stated proportions.

In deciding which beneficiaries are to suffer payable inheritance tax, you must bear in mind Section 41 of The Inheritance Tax Act 1984 which provides, in essence, that notwithstanding any provision of a will to the contrary, no exempt beneficiary shall be made to suffer the inheritance tax payable in respect of an exempt gift or exempt share of residue.

'Related property' valuation rules

When calculating whether or not a bequest will exceed the nil-rate band you must also bear in mind whether or not the Revenue will consider the subject of the bequest to be 'related property'. Related property is property which would have an increased value if owned with other property that is:

◆ owned by the taxpayer's spouse or civil partner; or

◆ was owned within the last five years by a charity, Housing Authority, political party which qualifies for exempt transfers, or an institution specified in the amended Schedule 3 of the

Inheritance Tax Act 1986 (roughly speaking bodies to which exempt transfers can be made such as national, local and university museums and art galleries, the National Trust and other bodies established for the preservation of the national heritage), to which it was transferred by the taxpayer or his spouse or civil partner after 15 April 1976.

An example will assist: suppose you own one of a set of three candelabra and your spouse owns the other two, the set of three will be worth more than treble the single candelabra, and even though you may have bought yours at an auction and your spouse inherited hers and, even if you propose to leave yours to your son and not to your spouse, the candelabra will be related property for inheritance tax purposes.

Related property is valued in special ways when calculating inheritance tax. There are what is known as the General Rule Method and the Special Rule Method. The General Rule Method is used when the items of related property have different attributes, e.g. the chairs and the table and the Special Rule method is used when the items are identical, such as shares of the same class of shares in a company which is an investment company and accordingly not entitled to business relief.

To ascertain the inheritance tax valuation of an asset using the General Rule Method, apportion the combined value of the assets in proportion to their value as separate items or, to put it another way, divide the asset's normal value by the total of its normal value and the normal value of the related property and multiply the result by their combined value.

To ascertain the inheritance tax valuation of an asset using the Special Rule Method, the apportionment is based upon the quantum and not the value of each asset. Therefore in the case of holdings of the same class of shares in a company it does not matter, for example, that one of the holdings is a majority shareholding and the other holding is a minority holding, (shares in a majority holding being worth more than shares in a minority holding); all that matters is the number of shares in each holding. To ascertain the value of a holding divide the number of shares held in the holding by the total number of shares in the holding and the related holding and multiply the result by the value of the combined holding.

Cohabitees and the survivor exemption

It is important to remember that in the case of *Holland v IRC* it was decided that for the purposes of inheritance tax the word 'spouse' only applies to those who are legally married and not to other cohabitees no matter how long cohabitees have been living together. The decision does not infringe the right to family life recognised by The European Convention on Human Rights or The Human Rights Act. Marriage and civil partnership involve the voluntary adoption of a body of legally recognised rights and obligations which clearly distinguish them from other forms of cohabitation. The Finance Act 2005 has changed the position to the extent that partners in a registered civil partnership have the benefit of the survivor exemption, but it still does not apply to other partners.

Long-term partners have been known to marry to obtain the spouse's inheritance tax exemption and widow's bereavement allowance.

Skipping a generation

If your children are wealthy you might wish to consider skipping a generation and instead of leaving bequests your children, leaving the bequests to or for the benefit of your grandchildren to avoid increased inheritance tax being payable on your children's deaths. In this way the bequest is only taxed once instead of twice before the grandchildren inherit it.

To skip a generation can also have income tax advantages if the grandchildren inherit before they become of age. The income tax advantage arises from the fact that if capital transferred to a child by a parent earns income in excess of £100 in any tax year, the income is taxed as if it were the parent's income, but income earned by capital transferred by a grandparent is treated as the grandchild's own income irrespective of the amount of the income and if it does not bring the grandchild's income above the grandchild's personal income tax allowance, any income tax deducted from the income can be recovered on behalf of the child.

Tax might also be saved when a beneficiary who is comfortably situated disclaims an inheritance so that it passes to his children and so skips a generation.

7

Clauses Recommended to be Included and Clauses Recommended to be Excluded from Your Will

YOUR NAME AND ADDRESS

It might seem simplistic to say so, but besides identifying the document as a will, the will should clearly state whose will it is. The usual way to identify the document as your will is to make sure that it says so by including your name and address but, as in most business matters, carelessness can cause confusion and in legal matters confusion equals expense. The first rule should be to give your true names and all your names, even though you do not normally use some of them or you are usually known by a nickname. Do not shorten a name, e.g. Beth for Elizabeth. If you have assets in a name which is not your true name, include that name as an alias. Thus the first sentence of your will might read, 'This is the last will of me Joseph Anthony Brown otherwise known as Tony Brown of 12 The Street Newtown Essex'. If a parent's names or a child's names are exactly the same as yours, include further identification by describing yourself as Junior or Senior or adding your occupation after your address. In the past, when men followed an occupation for life and women were not generally in employment, it was customary when drafting legal documents that a man should always be described by his occupation and a woman by her legal status such as married woman. Today this might be considered discriminatory.

THE DATE OF THE WILL

Always make certain that your will includes the date upon which it was signed and that codicils include their date and also refer to the date of the will to which they are a codicil. This is a great help if you omit to destroy an earlier will.

A REVOCATION CLAUSE

Include a clause to revoke earlier wills and codicils unless you wish the earlier document to stand as well as the one you are currently making. To avoid confusion, if you wish to make only a few additions or alterations to the earlier will, describe the new document as the first, or second as the case may be, codicil to your will dated [. . .]. If you wish to make numerous alterations it is better to revoke the earlier will and start afresh. It might be more convenient to have more than one subsisting will if each is to relate to property in a different country and they will need to be proved in different countries, but if you do so take care to ensure that the revocation clause in the later will is so worded that it does not inadvertently revoke the earlier will.

THE APPOINTMENT OF EXECUTORS

Chapter 4 has dealt with recommendations as to the number and choice of executors. Suffice it to say here that every will should appoint competent, trustworthy and willing executors who are likely to be available at the appropriate time.

ALTERNATIVE PROVISIONS FOR BEQUESTS TO BENEFICIARIES WHO PREDECEASE YOU AND FOR BEQUESTS THAT FAIL

If you make a bequest to someone and that person dies before you, your will will be treated as though it did not contain the bequest, the bequest will fail and the person's estate will not receive the bequest. In practical terms the effect of the beneficiary dying before you will be that the value of the residue of your estate will be increased by the amount of the bequest unless you include an alternative beneficiary for the gift in your will. If the bequest which fails is a bequest of a share of your residuary estate or of the entire residuary estate, unless you include an alternative beneficiary for the bequest, what is known as a partial intestacy will occur and, although the remainder of your will will take effect, you will be treated as though you have died intestate as far as the bequest is concerned and it will be dealt with according to the intestacy laws.

The same rules apply if a bequest fails for any other reason, for example because the bequest is contrary to the perpetuity law or contrary to public policy.

There are two exceptions to the above rules, namely gifts for charitable purposes which show an intention to benefit a charitable cause generally and not just a particular institution, and gifts which come within section 33 of the Wills Act 1837 as amended by the Administration of Justice Act 1982.

Charitable purposes are those defined by the Charities Act 2006. To qualify as charitable in the legal sense, a cause must have a substantial element of public benefit which will not be assumed and additionally be for one or more of the following purposes:

a. the relief of poverty;
b. the advancement of education;
c. the advancement of religion;

d. the advancement of health or the saving of lives;

e. the advancement of citizenship or community development;

f. the advancement of the arts, culture, heritage or science;

g. the advancement of amateur sport;

h. the advancement of human rights, conflict resolution or reconciliation or the promotion of religious harmony or equality and diversity;

i. the advancement of environmental protection or improvement;

j. the relief of those in need, by reason of youth, age, ill-health, disability, financial hardship or other disadvantage;

k. the advancement of animal welfare;

l. the promotion of the efficiency of the armed forces of the crown or the efficiency of the police, fire and rescue services or ambulance services;

m. any purpose:

    1. recognised as charitable under existing charity law; or

    2. reasonably regarded as analogous to or within the spirit of the above or existing charity law.

In the case of gifts to charity showing a general charitable intention such as a bequest to be used for research into a cure for a disease, if the charitable intention becomes impractical or impossible to carry out (for example once a cure has been found), a court will order that the bequest shall be used for the benefit of other charitable causes as similar as possible to those you intend unless your will shows a contrary intention.

The amended section 33 of the Wills Act provides that if you leave a gift to your child or other descendant such as a grandchild, and the proposed beneficiary dies before you but leaves a descendant who is living at your death, that first-generation descendant of the deceased beneficiary shall receive the bequest and it will not fail, unless your will shows a contrary intention. Illegitimacy is to be disregarded and any child who has been conceived before your death but born alive afterwards is treated as living at your death.

To avoid the complications, uncertainties and unexpected effects which can arise from the above rules it is better, within reason, to include an express provision in your will to provide what shall happen if your beneficiary dies before you. You can do this by stating that the bequest is given 'to X or if he shall die before me to Y' or you might decide to make the bequest 'to such of X, Y and Z as shall survive me and if more than one then equally between them'. Do not use the words 'in equal shares' unless you go on to state what is to happen to the share bequeathed to X, Y or Z if he dies before you. If you wish to leave the bequest to X, Y and Z in unequal shares, include words of accrual such as:

> I devise my farm in Devon as to one half thereof to X and as to one quarter thereof to each of Y and Z but if X Y or Z shall die before me the share of the said farm bequeathed to the person who dies before me shall not lapse but shall accrue and be added to the shares of those who survive me and if more than one pro rata so that they shall hold the farm in the same relative proportions.

Alternative wording could be:

> I devise my farm in Devon to my Trustees upon trust to divide the same into four equal shares and to hold two of such shares for X a further of such shares for Y and the

remaining share for Z provided that if any of the said X Y and Z shall die before me the share bequeathed to him shall not lapse but shall accrue and be added to the other share or shares the trusts of which have not failed.

Of course you may take the view that if a beneficiary dies before you, you will make a codicil or new will, but you might not have the chance if you lose your testamentary capacity or otherwise become seriously ill before, or soon after, your original beneficiary dies.

CLAUSES RELATING TO THE REMARRIAGE OF YOUR SPOUSE OR THE REGISTRATION OF YOUR CIVIL PARTNER'S NEW PARTNERSHIP AFTER YOUR DEATH AND PROVIDING FOR CHILDREN OF YOUR PREVIOUS MARRIAGE OR REGISTERED PARTNERSHIP

People are frequently concerned as to what will happen to their assets if they die and leave a spouse who remarries or a partner who enters into a new registered civil partnership after their death. They naturally do not wish their hard earned assets to be inherited via their spouse or partner by someone they have perhaps never even met and they wish to provide for their children as well as their spouse or partner. The problem is compounded by multiple relationships when the testator wishes to provide for the children of an earlier relationship as well as the second spouse or partner and perhaps children of the second relationship. Usually there are too many beneficiaries and not enough estate!

For the sake of easy reading I will write of spouses and marriage but the same points apply in this section to civil partners and registration of civil partnerships.

One possibility which you could consider is to leave your estate to your executors for your spouse during her lifetime or until she shall remarry and thereafter for your children. A problem with such a provision is that your spouse will only be able to spend the income produced by your estate, because if she spends capital, it will not be there to be inherited by the children after her death. Because many of the fixed outgoings which your spouse and yourself have during your joint lives will continue after your death, for example the costs of running your home, the income of your estate will be insufficient to provide a comfortable lifestyle unless it is supplemented by other income of your spouse or unless your estate is a large one.

Further possibilities that might be of assistance in part are

- to leave non-income bearing assets to the children;

- to leave the matrimonial home to your surviving spouse only during her remaining life;

- to leave the matrimonial home to her only during her widowhood; or

- to leave your estate to your executors and provide that they shall hold it upon a discretionary trust for your spouse and the children and/or other chosen beneficiaries so that the trustees can make payments from the estate to the trust beneficiaries in the trustees' discretion and according to the beneficiaries' needs as the trustees see them.

If you leave the matrimonial home to your spouse for life, it could cause problems for your spouse's second husband after her death, unless the second husband has his own funds out of which he could buy the home from the children or unless he has an alternative home.

By statute there is a presumption that makes an absolute gift of property in your will or codicil to your spouse and an interest in the property for your issue ineffective, as far as the gift to your issue is concerned, unless the document shows a contrary intention. Accordingly to say 'I give my house to my wife' and later to say 'I give my house to my son' will give your son nothing and it is necessary to say 'I give my house to my wife for the remainder of her life and after her death to my son', or words to that effect.

If you choose to leave the matrimonial home to your spouse for life or only during her widowhood or to set up a discretionary trust, you should ensure that you fully understand the tax implications and it is better to have your will drawn up by a professional who is experienced in tax and in the law of wills. You will also need to consider how the furnishings are to be left. If a life interest in the furnishings is to be given, provide that the executors shall take an inventory of the furnishings and of their condition at the date of your death and state who is to bear the cost of insuring them. The problem discussed in this section of the book can be discussed with your spouse and if a reciprocal agreement is reached, mutual wills as discussed in Chapter 3 can be entered into to ensure that the desired result is achieved and one spouse does not cheat upon the other after the first death.

However you propose to leave your estate, you should always bear in mind the Inheritance (Provision for Family and Dependants) Act 1975 which was referred to in Chapter 3.

MIRROR/MUTUAL WILLS

In Chapter 3 I have written extensively on the subject of mirror wills and mutual wills and I suggest that you refer back to that section and decide whether or not it is appropriate for you to include a declaration in your will as to whether it is a mutual will or a mirror will or whether such a declaration can be safely omitted. If a declaration is included but no separate mutual wills agreement entered into, your will should also be signed by the maker of the other will.

WHO BEARS THE DEBTS, FUNERAL EXPENSES AND EXPENSES INCURRED IN CARRYING OUT YOUR WILL AND INHERITANCE TAX?

Always make sure that you have made it clear in your will from which parts of your estate you intend your debts, funeral expenses and expenses incurred in carrying out your will shall be paid. In Chapter 6 I have dealt with the circumstances in which legacies are grossed up in calculating inheritance tax and I suggest you refer back to that chapter to decide whether your legacies should be given free of tax or subject to tax.

Inheritance tax in respect of lifetime gifts made less than seven years before you die and inheritance tax on joint or foreign property is borne by the person who receives the property or gift and not by those who inherit your residuary estate, but unless you state otherwise in your will tax on any other kind of property is borne by those who inherit your residuary estate with the exceptions of your surviving spouse, or your surviving registered civil partner and registered charities. They can never be made to bear the inheritance tax.

GIVING PROPERTY WHICH IS MORTGAGED OR SUBJECT TO A FINANCIAL CHARGE

If you leave property which is mortgaged or security for any other debt such as a local authority charge for unpaid road charges or the cost of keeping a relative in a local authority home, the debt must be paid primarily out of that property unless you show a contrary intention in your will. Merely stating that all your debts are to be paid out of your residuary estate does not in itself show a sufficient contrary intention and you should say that the gift of the property is 'free from all mortgages and all charges subsisting in respect of it at the date of my death'.

GIVING LIFETIME INTERESTS IN ASSETS

If you leave a building such as your house to someone only for their life, do not forget that you will need to decide who is to be responsible for maintaining the property and paying the outgoings and expenses of occupation such as council tax, water rates and sewage charges, and to set this out in your will. Are such items to be borne by the life tenant or by your residuary estate? Your executors will find it helpful if you insert in your will a clause 'I GIVE my executors an absolute and unfettered discretion as to how they allocate the expenses of administering and maintaining assets of my estate between the capital and the income of my estate'. In the absence of any such clause, expenses incurred for the benefit of the entire estate must be charged to the capital of the estate and expenses which can be shown to relate exclusively to income can be deducted from the estate's income but the burden of proving that an expense relates solely to income is upon your executors.

Remember that a life tenant of a property is entitled to live in the property or to have the benefit of the net income produced by the property during their life. Similarly the life tenant of any other trust fund is entitled to the net income produced by the trust fund during their life. If you are thinking of leaving a life interest by your will, consider whether it might be a better idea, in the particular circumstances, to use the principles set out in Chapter 4 in connection with spendthrifts and discretionary trusts and protective trusts instead. You would do this by not leaving the property to the beneficiary for life, but only until the beneficiary dies or goes into a nursing or residential home for the elderly as the beneficiary's normal residence (whichever happens first). This would prevent the income being taken into account by the local authority in assessing contributions to fees. If you decide to do this you will need to consult a professional lawyer for advice and to draft the will.

ADDITIONAL ADMINISTRATIVE POWERS IN WILLS

There are certain powers the general law does not give to your executors but which you can give to them by expressly including a clause in your will to oil the wheels and make their task of carrying out your wishes much easier. Equally there are powers which the general law gives to your executors which you might not wish them to have and which you can expressly exclude by clauses in your will. I will discuss some of these powers below and include specimens of such clauses in the appendix.

Powers of maintenance and advancement in relation to contingent gifts and gifts to minors

If you make a gift to a person which is only to take effect upon the occurrence of a contingency or a gift to a person who is under age, there are statutory and common law powers for your executors to use part of the gift for the maintenance or other benefit of the person concerned before the contingency fulfilled or the beneficiary has come of age. The powers are hedged around with complex restrictions and limitations and it is better to give your executors flexibility by including a simpler and wider express clause in your will.

Powers of investment and borrowing

If there is the possibility that the administration of your estate will continue for some time after your death, for example if by your will you leave a life interest or bequests which are contingent upon the happening of some event such as a beneficiary attaining a particular age, you should consider giving your executors wide powers to invest the assets of your estate and to borrow upon them. The powers otherwise given to them by law are cumbersome.

Receipt clauses for bequests to minors and bequests to organisations

Unless you insert a specific clause in your will to authorise it, a minor has no power to give a receipt for a bequest and unless the minor is married or in a registered civil partnership he cannot give a valid receipt for any income it produces. Therefore, if you have left a bequest to a minor, unless you include a suitable receipt clause, your executors will be unable to hand over the bequest until the beneficiary attains his majority or unless an expensive application is successfully made to a court to vary the will; if they do so the beneficiary might be allowed to claim and receive the bequest a second time upon reaching the age of 18 and your executors will have to carry the can. In appropriate circumstances a suitable receipt clause would be one that allows your executors to obtain a valid discharge and receipt from parents or others as trustees for the bequest of the minor.

If you leave a bequest to an organisation such as a charity, it makes life simpler for your executors if you include a clause in your will stating specifically which officers of the organisation can give your executors a valid receipt and discharge for the bequest.

Beneficiaries who cannot be found

Sometimes, in spite of all their best efforts, your executors may not be able to find beneficiaries who are named in your will. Section 27 of the Trustee Act 1925 provides that in such a case your executors shall be free to distribute the estate having regard only to claims of which they have notice after making certain searches and giving 'such notices as would, in any special case, have been directed by a court of competent jurisdiction in an action for administration'. Rather than putting your executors at risk or compelling them to protect themselves by putting your estate to the expense of asking a court what notices it directs should be given, it is better to include in your will a clause setting out a simpler procedure for dealing with the interests of missing beneficiaries.

Limited interests and apportionment of income

If you are leaving a bequest by your will to someone during the beneficiary's lifetime or for a limited period, your executors will find it very helpful if you insert a clause which relieves them of any obligation to apportion, between the beneficiary and those who subsequently become entitled to the bequest, any income which arises from the bequest and straddles the limited and subsequent periods. This is particularly the case if you leave the beneficiary a life interest in the estate and the executors invest the estate in a spread of investments to minimise risk.

Apportionment of expenses

Your executors will find it helpful if you insert in your will a clause giving them an absolute and unfettered discretion as to how they allocate the expenses of administering and maintaining assets of your estate between the capital and the income of the estate. In the absence of any such clause, expenses incurred for the benefit of the entire estate must be charged to the capital of the estate and expenses which can be shown to relate exclusively to income can be deducted from the estate's income but the burden of proving that an expense relates solely to income is upon your executors.

Giving your executor power to carry on a business

A personal representative's power to invest in or carry on a business is hedged around with restrictions and conditions and unless they are complied with it should be wound up and that should be done within one year. If the business is carried on for longer than one year without complying with the restrictions the personal representatives are personally liable for any debts and losses incurred. If you run or are likely to run a business, consider giving your executors power to carry on either alone or in partnership any business in which you are involved as a partner or proprietor at the date of your death and provide that they shall be entitled to be indemnified out your estate for any debts or liabilities reasonably incurred in carrying on the business. A specimen clause can be found in the appendix.

Giving your executor power to buy from your estate

An executor has no right to buy property from your estate even though he may offer a good price for it or buy it at auction, unless you authorise him to do so by your will.

Giving powers to appoint new or additional trustees

After your will has been proved your executors can appoint new trustees to act jointly with them in the administration of your estate should that be necessary, but if you wish you can give that power to someone else.

Excluding the beneficiaries' power to remove trustees

In essence Section 19 of The Trusts of Land and Appointment of Trustees Act 1996 gives beneficiaries who are together absolutely entitled to trust property and legally competent, power to replace existing trustees with new trustees of the beneficiaries' choice, provided that there is no one still alive who was given power by the will to appoint new trustees. If you do not wish your trustees to have the power to remove the executor trustees you have chosen, exclude the application of this section from your will. The section applies to all trusts unless it is excluded and not just to trusts of land.

Excluding the duty of trustees of land to consult with beneficiaries

Section 11(1) of The Trusts of Land and Appointment of Trustees Act 1996 reads 'The trustees of land shall in the exercise of any function relating to land subject to the trust:

(a) so far as is practicable, consult the beneficiaries of full age and beneficially entitled to an interest in possession in the land; and

(b) so far as is consistent with the general interest of the trust, give effect to the wishes of those beneficiaries, or in the case of dispute of the majority (according to their combined interests).'

This section is vague and uncertain in several respects: what is 'the general interest' of the trust and under what circumstances is

it not 'practicable' to consult? Uncertainty leads to d..,
legal disputes are expensive. It is better to exclude the section
from the operation of your will. Your trustees do not need
statutory authority to authorise them to consult affected
beneficiaries before taking major decisions and they are probably
always wise to do so in case they are later sued over the decision,
whether or not they have a duty to do so. If you trust your
trustees, it is better not to fetter their powers. If you do not trust
them, appoint someone else instead.

Limiting the extent of liability for acts done in the administration of your estate

You might wish to consider including a clause in your will to
exempt non-professional executors from legal liability for their
acts and omissions in the administration of your estate unless the
acts constitute fraud or gross negligence. Without such a clause
such executors, who are unlikely to be insured against negligence
in the performance of executorship duties, might well be
unwilling to accept the position. Everyone makes mistakes from
time to time. Such a clause will not be void on the grounds of
public policy, even if the executor drew up the will for you.

Attestation clause
Your will should always include what is known as an attestation
clause, i.e. a clause which explains the circumstances in which it was
signed and witnessed to show that they comply with the
requirements of the Wills Act.

Settling old scores
Finally, do not attempt to settle old scores by your will. The
probate document will omit anything which is libellous or
blasphemous.

8

Points on Which You Should Take Special Care When Drafting Your Will

BE PRECISE AND SAY WHAT YOU MEAN

Do not use phrases such as 'I hope that', 'I trust that', or 'I request'; be definite if you intend your wishes to be carried out.

Be precise and avoid vague wording which will make gifts fail to take effect by reason of a lack of certainty. It is much safer to take care and state your intentions unambiguously rather than rely upon someone attempting to guess them. The devil himself knoweth not the mind of man – or of woman either if it comes to that!

The courts will lean over backwards to give effect to your intentions but they will not make your will for you. They will start to seek your intentions by giving the words you have used their natural i.e. ordinary, meaning, having regard to the contents of your will looked at as a whole. They will give some, but very little, attention to what specific words have been held to mean in previous cases. Sometimes evidence to show that the words used had a special meaning for you can be considered but courts have very limited powers to look beyond the wording of your will to ascertain your intention. They are only permitted to do so if the wording of the will is meaningless or shown to be ambiguous on the face of the will or in the light of surrounding circumstances. If this is not so and the wording of your will appears to show your intentions clearly, the courts have no power to hear evidence as to what you actually intended and must give effect to your wishes *as expressed* in your will, even though external evidence would have shown that the wording of your will did not express your wishes correctly.

If your intention in any part of your will is not clear after taking into account any external evidence it is permitted to consider, a court must ignore that part of the will and it will not take effect. You must therefore make your meaning absolutely clear and unambiguous at all times. It is so easy to think, incorrectly, that because you know what you mean, that is what you have written and it is a good idea to have someone read over your will for you to see if they are clear about what you intend and to check that what they think you intend is in fact what you intend. If you do not make it clear what you intend to give and who you intend shall benefit from the gift, the gift may well fail to take effect completely by reason of uncertainty.

If a court is satisfied, after considering the evidence it is permitted to consider, that the wording of your will does not carry out your intentions because of a clerical error or the failure of the draftsman (if it was prepared for you by someone else) to understand the intentions, it can rectify your will so as to carry out your intentions. Although a court can interpret the meaning of the words of your will, it cannot rectify the wording of your will for any other reason. It cannot, for example, rectify your will because you did not appreciate the inheritance tax effects of your intended bequest. Rectification is only available to correct the way your intentions have been recorded and not their substance.

A striking example of the lengths to which a court will go to use its power to rectify a will to achieve a testator's intention is the case of

Vautier's Estate. The facts were that a husband and wife signed each other's wills by mistake, the wills having been prepared in reciprocal terms. The mistake did not come to light until after the wife's death. The court decided that the will she had not signed could not be proved as her will, because she had not signed it and completed it in accordance with the required formalities. However, the will she had signed would be rectified to carry out her perceived intention and was allowed to be proved as her will after the wording had been amended. Although this was a Jersey case it is thought that the result would be the same in England or Wales.

DESCRIBING BENEFICIARIES

Describe beneficiaries by their full correct names rather than merely using their relationship to you, and give their addresses. This will be of assistance to your executors, not only in identifying the beneficiaries, but also in tracing them. If this is not possible because you intend to benefit a fluctuating group of people identified by description, such as your nephews, specify a cut-off date. Take care to say whether you intend to include only members of that group who are living at the date of your will or also those born after the date of your will and before your death. Any person conceived but not born at the date of your death is considered to be living. If you wish to include members of a group who are born after your death, remember that it will not be possible to distribute your bequest until it is no longer possible for anyone else to join the group covered by the description.

Remember also the complicated rules of the Perpetuity and Accumulations Act 1964 (dealt with in more detail later in this chapter) and that in case the Act should invalidate the bequest, it is safer not to make any gift by your will in respect of which gift all the beneficiaries will not have been ascertained and qualified for their share of the bequest within 21 years of your death.

If you leave a bequest to relatives by the description of their relationship to you, such as nieces, nephews, uncles or aunts, make it clear whether you intend to include only blood relatives or whether you intend to include relatives by marriage, (e.g. the daughters of your wife's sister as your nieces) and by civil partnership registration.

Remember that the Gender Recognition Act 2004 means that a change of gender will be recognised in respect of wills made after, but not wills made before, the Act came into force if a Gender Recognition Certificate has been issued; a bequest to your nieces, for example will therefore be considered to include someone who was born as your nephew and has obtained a certificate. It is true that a court has power under the Act to make such order as it considers to be appropriate and just but it is safer to name the beneficiaries if possible rather to rely upon a court correctly guessing your intentions.

A gift to your 'issue' or 'descendants' will mean that each of such people who are living at the date of your death will inherit an equal share. If this is not what you intend and your intention is that any such person shall inherit only if their ancestors who are your descendants have all died before you, make your gift to your 'descendants per stirpes'. (Please refer to the explanations of 'Gifts per stirpes' and 'Gifts per capita' in the glossary.)

A gift to your children will be taken to include your adopted and your illegitimate children (if any), but not your stepchildren unless you indicate in your will that that is not your intention or you have no other children at the date of the will, but any person who has been treated as a child of your family in respect of your marriage, your former marriage or registered civil partnership will have a right to make a claim for reasonable provision from your estate under the Inheritance (Provision for Family and Dependants) Act 1975, as amended.

The words 'relations' or 'next of kin' will usually be taken to mean those who will inherit your estate if you die intestate. (Please refer to Chapter 1.)

There is no provision in the Civil Partnership Act for the word 'spouse' to include 'Civil Partner' and accordingly 'spouse' in a will will usually not be read as 'Civil Partner'.

Do not use nicknames. A bequest to 'mother' led to litigation where a testator was in the habit of calling his wife 'mother' and both the wife and natural mother were living at his death.

If you make a gift to charity, identify it by its exact name and registered number and say that the gift is made for its charitable purposes. In a case in which the charity was in the course of liquidation at the date of the testator's death and the will did not say that the gift is made for its charitable purposes, the court decided that the gift took effect for the benefit of the charity's creditors and did not have the benefit of inheritance tax relief because the creditors were not a charitable purpose.

If you intend that your gift shall be for the benefit of a particular branch of the charity, say so or the gift will go to the head office of the charity.

The registered number of a charity can be obtained directly from the charity or from the Charity Commission at PO Box 1277, Liverpool L69 3UG. Telephone: 0845 3000 218. Website: *www.charity-commission.gov.uk.*

To understand what will happen to any bequest to a beneficiary who dies before you or a bequest which fails to take effect for any other reason, if you have made no alternative provision in your will, please refer to the section in Chapter 7 headed 'Alternative provisions for bequests to beneficiaries who predecease you and for bequests that fail'.

DESCRIBING BEQUESTS

In the same way as it is necessary to be precise when describing beneficiaries it is necessary to avoid uncertainty when describing what you intend to give.

Do not use vague phrases such as 'a substantial legacy', 'fair recompense', 'some of my'.

If you have several items that fit a description, e.g. several tea services, do not say merely 'my tea service'; rather particularise the item further by saying, for example, 'my Royal Doulton carnation patterned tea service'.

It is not a good idea to include a large number of bequests of individual items in your will; you might not own them at your death and your beneficiaries might feel embarrassed to decline or discard them but not really want them. If you give a legacy of, say, a car, make it clear as to whether the legacy refers to the car you own now or to any car you might own at the date of your death.

Similarly it is not a good idea to leave a particular bank or building society account or the money in such an account as a bequest; the balance in the account at any particular time will vary and when you die at some (hopefully) long time in the future, the account might have been closed.

Describe property by its postal address 'and the land and premises occupied therewith'.

Make it clear whether any bequest you make is given 'subject to tax', in which case the beneficiary bears any inheritance tax payable in respect of it, or 'free of tax', in which case the tax is payable by your residuary estate unless the residuary estate is left to an exempt beneficiary. In the absence of any provision to the contrary in your will, tax in respect of joint or foreign property will be borne by the beneficiary, but tax in respect of other property left by your will will be borne by your residuary estate, again unless the residuary estate is left to an exempt beneficiary.

If you wish to leave a bequest to your executor or to someone who is a trustee under your will for their own benefit, state that the bequest is given to them 'absolutely'.

A bequest of something which you do not own at the date of your death will not take effect except in the special circumstances of the doctrine of election discussed in Chapter 3 under the heading

'Other property you do not own over which you have no power of appointment'.

Bequeathing something by your will does not prevent you from subsequently disposing of it later in your lifetime to the beneficiary or to any other person.

LEGACIES TO THOSE WHO OWE YOU MONEY AND TO THOSE TO WHOM YOU OWE MONEY

If you leave a bequest to someone who owes you money, make it clear in your will as to whether you intend that the legacy shall be paid and the debt forgiven or whether the debt shall be deducted from the legacy.

If you leave a legacy to a creditor, make it clear whether you intend the legacy to be in substitution for or in addition to the debt.

THE VALUE OF YOUR LEGACIES

Take care to ensure that the total value of the legacies you have bequeathed does not exceed the likely value of your estate calculated *after* making provision for any payable inheritance tax, your funeral expenses and the expense of administering your estate. Every individual legacy or bequest you make reduces the amount available to the beneficiaries of your residuary estate. If your estate is insufficient to pay all your debts, funeral expenses, the cost of administering the estate and to meet the bequests or your estate is insolvent when you die, the law imposes complex rules as to the order and extent to which each shall be paid.

THE MEANING OF SOME WORDS AND PHRASES

Do not attempt to use technical terms in your will if ordinary words will do.

In order to achieve your intentions as expressed in your will, the courts will take a practical and common sense view in giving effect to your intentions and interpret words according to the context in which you use them, but it can be useful to know how they have been interpreted in the past.

The words 'family' and 'my relations' have been variously interpreted and if possible it is better not to use these words.

'Next of kin': the phrase 'next of kin' is usually interpreted in accordance with the order set out for inheritance on intestacy (see Chapter 1).

'My money' has been variously interpreted according to its context in the will as a whole and might be taken as referring only to cash, or on the other hand to include bank accounts or investments: it is better not to use the term without further amplification.

'My personal estate', 'my personal effects', 'my goods and chattels' or 'my belongings' are usually taken to include all your moveable items, but not your freehold or leasehold property. However, 'my estate' or 'my possessions' is usually construed as meaning all your assets including non-moveable property.

'Personal' estate or 'personal' chattels will not usually be construed to include items used for business purposes.

A useful and comprehensive, if somewhat dated, definition of personal chattels can be found in section 55 (1) (x) of the Administration of Estates Act 1925:

> 'Personal chattels' mean carriages, horses, stable furniture and effects (not used for business purposes), motor cars and accessories (not used for business purposes), garden effects, domestic animals, plate, plated articles, linen, china, glass, books, pictures, prints, furniture, jewellery, articles of household or personal use or ornament, musical and scientific instruments and apparatus, wines, liquors and consumable stores, but do not include any chattels used at the death...for business purposes nor money or securities for money.

Note that the definition includes pets for which you may wish to make separate alternative provision in your will.

This definition can be incorporated in your will if you wish by providing 'I bequeath my personal chattels as defined by section 55(1)(x) of the Administration of Estates Act 1925 to...'.

If you wish to amend and update it to include, for example electronic equipment and/or boats, or to exclude any items, it can be amended and then copied in full into the will.

'Furniture' said Lord Justice Stamp in the case of *Crispin's Will Trusts, Re Arkwright v Thurley* means 'something which contributed to the use of, enjoyment or convenience of the house'

'Jewellery' includes unmounted precious stones but 'personal jewellery' is usually considered to mean jewellery which is mounted ready to be worn personally.

After a change of gender has taken place and a Gender Recognition Certificate has been issued under the Gender Recognition Act of 2004 it will be recognised in relation to wills made after the Act so that your transsexual brother will usually inherit under a gift to 'my sisters'. However under section 18 of the Act a court has power to make such order as it considers appropriate and just in the case of a person benefiting from a disposition of property as a result of the Act.

'Month' means calendar month unless lunar month or four weeks is specifically stated.

'From' a date does not include the date.

However, I repeat that the meaning of the words you use will always be decided according to the context in which they are used looking at the will and your individual way of life as a whole. An example is that a stamp collection acquired by a testator as his main hobby was held by a court to be an article 'of personal use' but if it had been acquired purely as an investment it would have been considered to be a business asset.

VOID PROVISIONS IN WILLS

Earlier in this chapter I explained that an attempted bequest will fail if the subject of the bequest or the beneficiary to whom it is given is not described in such a way that it is certain. Your bequest may also fail because it falls within the following kinds of gifts:

Gifts to those who witness your will

You need only two witnesses to the signing of your will or codicil, but if you leave a bequest to one of the witnesses or to the spouse or civil partner of one of the witnesses, although the choice of witness will not invalidate your will, the choice of witness will invalidate the bequest and it will not take effect unless the witness's signature can be regarded as superfluous because you have used two other disinterested witnesses. To avoid problems do not choose beneficiaries or the spouses or civil partners of beneficiaries as witnesses to your signature.

Gifts which are contrary to law or contrary to public policy

If you include a bequest in your will which the law considers to be contrary to law or public policy, the gift will not achieve your wishes. If the bequest is considered to be essentially evil, e.g. a bequest conditional upon murdering someone, the bequest will fail completely, but if the condition upon which the bequest is given is merely prohibited by law or public policy, only the condition will be void. If you intend that the gift shall only take effect if the condition is fulfilled, i.e. the condition is what is known as a *condition precedent* and the condition is void, the gift will fail completely, but if you intended that the gift shall take effect but cease if the condition is fulfilled, i.e. the condition is what is known as a *condition subsequent*, the gift will take effect free from the void condition. An example of a gift with a condition precedent is a gift to your son if he successfully completes the university course he is taking and an example of a condition subsequent is a gift to him,

but if he fails the course, then to your daughter, although both of
these conditions are of course valid ones.

You must distinguish between conditions (which may or may not
be valid) and limitations which are restrictions upon the period of
ownership, i.e. gifts until an event occurs, which are always valid.

Exactly what is considered to be contrary to public policy changes
from time to time but a few principles can be stated.

◆ Gifts that weaken the family unit or the institution of marriage
  are contrary to public policy. Therefore if you leave a gift to
  your son if he leaves his wife the gift will not take effect
  because it is a condition which is void being both contrary to
  public policy and a condition precedent.

◆ Conditions contrary to the inherent legal nature of property, e.g.
  that a property shall not be sold or shall be boarded up and not
  used for a long specified time, are contrary to public policy.

◆ Conditions which interfere with the right of a parent to control
  the education or religious upbringing of his child are contrary
  to public policy.

If you provide in your will that a bequest is to be forfeited if the
beneficiary challenges the will, such a provision is enforceable and
not considered to be contrary to public policy, but it will not be
considered to have been breached by a beneficiary instituting
proceedings to protect his rights. Also, the bequest might fail to
take effect for reasons of uncertainty, unless the relevant clause is
carefully drafted.

Gifts which infringe the rules against perpetuities accumulations

The law contains very complex rules (mainly contained in the Perpetuities and Accumulations Act 1964), which prevent the income from a bequest being accumulated and added to the capital of the bequest by the personal representatives for an excessive period, rather than distributed to the beneficiary, and which also prevent bequests being made to beneficiaries whose identity might not be ascertained for an excessively long time in the future. These rules are known as the rules against perpetuities and accumulations. If you wish to make a bequest and the identity of the beneficiary might not be ascertained within 21 years of your death, e.g. a gift 'to my grandchildren whether born before or after my death', or a gift dependent upon the fulfilling of a condition which might not be fulfilled within 21 years of your death, be sure to consult a solicitor about the wording and to check whether it can be legally done. Similarly, if you wish the income of a bequest to be accumulated for a period that could exceed 21 years, consult a solicitor.

SECTION 33 OF THE WILLS ACT 1837, AS AMENDED

By this section, if you leave a gift to a descendant and that beneficiary dies before you but leaves his descendant who is living at your death, the bequest will take effect as a bequest to the descendant who is living at your death, unless your will shows a contrary intention. If it is not your intention that the bequest shall be construed in this way make your intention clear, for example by stating expressly what is to happen to the bequest if your nominated beneficiary predeceases you.

THE EFFECT OF DIVORCE OR ANNULMENT OF YOUR MARRIAGE OR DISSOLUTION OF YOUR CIVIL PARTNERSHIP ON YOUR WILL

The effect on bequests to your spouse or civil partner

Dissolution of your marriage or civil partnership does not invalidate your will, but a decree absolute (not a decree nisi) makes any bequest in the will to your spouse or civil partner as the case may be take effect as if the former spouse or partner had died on the date the decree becomes absolute, leaving bequests in the remainder of your will valid. Usually the bequest will become part of the residue of your estate and go to your residuary beneficiaries, but if the bequest is of the entire estate or of a share of the residue of the estate, it will be treated as not having been disposed of by your will and will be inherited on your death according to the laws of intestacy.

The effect on your spouse's or partner's power of appointment, executorship and trusteeship

Similarly, any provisions in your will conferring powers of appointment on your spouse or partner (i.e. power for him to appoint or choose a beneficiary for part of an estate) or appointing him as an executor or trustee take effect after a decree absolute of dissolution of your marriage or civil partnership as if the former spouse or partner had died on the date the decree became absolute.

The effect on your spouse or partner as guardian

Unless a contrary intention is apparent from your will, an appointment of your spouse or civil partner as a guardian of an under-age child is revoked by a decree absolute of divorce, annulment or dissolution which either is made in a court in England or Wales or would be recognised by such a court.

The effect upon any Enduring or Lasting Power of Attorney you have made

Unless the Enduring Power of Attorney or Lasting Power of Attorney states that it is not to do so, the dissolution or annulment of your marriage or civil partnership terminates the appointment of your spouse or civil partner as your attorney under any Enduring Power of Appointment that you have given. Similarly unless the Enduring Power of Attorney provides that it is not to do so, the dissolution or annulment of your marriage or civil partnership revokes the power unless your spouse or civil partner is replaced under the terms of the power or he is one of several donees appointed to act jointly and severally and after the event there is at least one remaining donee.

Because the above effects only occur on a decree absolute, take care to make a new will as soon as it is clear that your partnership or marriage has irretrievably broken down, because if you die before decree absolute, any will you have will stand and if you merely revoke your will, your estate will be distributed as though you were intestate.

9

The International Element of Wills

In these days of easy travel, holidays abroad, comparative affluence, early retirement, armed conflicts and the globalisation of business, it is becoming increasingly common for people to own property, work and retire in countries other than those in which they were born. In these circumstances, consideration of how foreign factors can affect your will is becoming increasingly important.

THE FORMALITIES FOR COMPLETING A VALID WILL IF YOU ARE OUTSIDE ENGLAND AND WALES

The formalities that have to be followed to make a valid will if you are in England or Wales have been dealt with in Chapter 2. If you make a will without observing those formalities while you are abroad, English law will accept it as validly made if it is made

♦ in accordance with the formalities required by the state where it was made; or

♦ in accordance with the formalities required by the state where at the time the will was made or at your death you were domiciled or had your habitual residence or of which you were a national. The meaning of 'domicile' has been explained in Chapter 3.

If the will deals with immoveable property such as a holiday villa, it will also be recognised as valid by English law as regards that property if it complies with the formalities required by the law of the state in which the property is situated.

If you make your will on a ship or aircraft the will will also be treated as validly completed if its completion conforms to the law of the country with which the ship or aircraft has the closest connection.

An alternative provision to validate wills made abroad was provided by the Convention providing for a Uniform Law on the Form of an International Will. The provisions of this convention will be incorporated into English law by the section 28 of the Administration of Justice Act 1982 when the section is brought into force by a commencement order. Unfortunately, although the convention has been adopted by parts of Canada, by Ecuador, Libya, Niger, Portugal and the former Yugoslavia, and the Act was passed over 20 years ago, no commencement order appears to have been made. As mentioned in Chapter 1, such matters do not rank highly upon the political agenda.

For your will to be valid under the convention:

◆ The will must be made in writing.   *outside England*

◆ You must declare in front of an 'authorised person' and two other witnesses that the document is your will and that you are aware of its contents and you must sign the will at the end of the will or acknowledge your signature, in either case, in their presence.

◆ The authorised person and the witnesses must immediately sign at the end of the will in your presence to attest it.

◆ If the will consists of more than one page, each page must be numbered and signed by the authorised person and yourself.

♦ The authorised person must prepare a certificate in the prescribed form to the effect that the formalities have been complied with.

WILLS RELATING TO PROPERTY WHICH IS SITUATED OUTSIDE OF ENGLAND AND WALES

The previous section dealt with the formalities to be followed when making a will abroad if it is to be recognised as valid in English law, but when considering any property you may have which is situated abroad, you must also consider the foreign law relating to the property and the making of wills, even if the will is made in the United Kingdom. Some states have restrictions in relation to who can inherit property and the tax laws relating to property differ from those of English law. The procedure and formalities for making a will that is to be recognised by the foreign country as a valid document of title to the property are usually different from those of England and Wales. It is usually better to make a will in the country where the property is situated to deal with foreign property, or at least to obtain advice from a lawyer who practises in the law of the relevant country.

You can have several valid wills at the same time and separate wills dealing with different parts of your estate, e.g. a will covering your English property and a separate will covering your foreign property. Making a will in England or Wales to deal with your assets in these countries and separate wills in foreign countries to deal with your assets in those countries, speeds up the issue of Probate and other required grants of representation and the administration of your estate. If you do so, make sure that the foreign will does not contain a clause revoking your English will or any codicil, and similarly make sure that your English documents do not revoke the foreign will. A clause in the later will such as 'I revoke all wills and testamentary documents previously made by me' would revoke the other will. Take care in each will to make it clear that the English property/the foreign property/the will, as appropriate, is excluded from the revocation clause.

INTERPRETING WILLS THAT HAVE A FOREIGN ELEMENT

A will is interpreted according to the law of the country intended by the testator and in the absence of any indication to the contrary that law is presumed to be the law of the country in which the testator was domiciled when the will was made.

10

Revoking or Amending Your Will

AMENDING YOUR WILL

You can amend or revoke your will and you can make a new will at any time if you have the necessary mental capacity to do so. If you make an error when you are typing or writing out your will, it is better to destroy it and start again, but if you decide that to do so would be too inconvenient, you can cross out the offending word or words or, if appropriate make an interlineation or insertion, but whatever you decide to do make sure that after the alteration the will remains legible and your meaning is clear and unambiguous. All alterations must be initialled, first by you and then by those who witness your signature and before the final signing process is completed, to show that the alterations were made *before* the will was completed. If the alterations are not initialled in this way and the original writing is still legible, a court will give effect to the will in its unaltered form, but if the alterations are not initialled and the original wording has been obliterated and is illegible, both the original and the altered wording will be ignored and the will will take effect as if there is a blank space in the will.

If you decide that you wish to change your will after you have made it, ideally you should revoke the will and make a new will, but if the changes are minor, such as deleting or adding a beneficiary, guardian or executor, you can do so by making a codicil to your Will. A codicil is a separate supplementary document which adds to or varies an existing testamentary document; a specimen form of codicil is to be found in the appendix to this book. If you do make a codicil, be certain to read it over in conjunction with the will and any codicils you may have made earlier to be sure that the provisions of the documents do not conflict. Codicils must be signed and witnessed in accordance with the rules set out in Chapter 2 for the signing of wills, but your will and its codicils need not have the same witnesses.

REVOKING YOUR WILL

The privileged wills of those engaged in actual military service and sailors at sea

In the same way as you can make a will at any age and orally or without any formalities if you are one of the above persons, you can similarly revoke your will at any age and orally or without any formalities if you come within the above classes.

If you do not come within one of the above classes your will will only be revoked in one of the following ways.

Revocation by marriage or registration of a civil partnership

With the exception of what is said below in respect of the exercise of a power of appointment by will if you have an existing will when you enter into a valid marriage or civil partnership, the mere fact of the marriage or partnership will revoke the will unless the will shows that it was made with that particular marriage or partnership in mind and you do not intend it to revoke the will. The will may show your intention in respect of the person concerned either by expressly saying so or by clear implication, such as referring to him as your fiancée or future husband or partner.

If you wish the will to be effective only if the event takes place, say in the will that it is to be conditional upon it taking place within a specified period, for example, a year. If a will apparently made with a particular marriage or partnership registration in mind is not made conditional upon the marriage or partnership registration taking place within a specified period it will be effective until it is revoked by one or more of the other methods of revoking wills irrespective of whether or not the marriage takes place or the partnership registration is made before you die.

Marriage to or registration of a partnership with one person will, of course, revoke a will which states that it is made in contemplation of marriage or partnership with a different person.

Any appointment of property which you make by your will in the exercise of a power of appointment which you have will not be revoked if you subsequently enter a civil partnership or marry unless the property would form part of your estate if you had not made the appointment.

Revoking your will by destroying it with the intention to revoke it

Your will will be revoked if it is destroyed by you or by another person at your request and in your presence. In either case you must intend that the will shall be revoked.

The formalities must be strictly followed and you must have the requisite intention. It is not sufficient to write 'revoked' on the will or to cross out part of the will. If the will is only partially destroyed or obliterated, e g by tearing a piece out of the will, unless that piece is a vital part of the will, only the part torn out or obliterated will be revoked and the rest of the will will remain valid. Neither is it sufficient if you accidentally destroy the will or if you are so drunk that you do not know what you are doing when you do it or you otherwise lack mental capacity. Moreover, if you ask someone to destroy your will for you, the destruction will be ineffective unless it is done in your presence: for this purpose presence is narrowly interpreted and it is not sufficient if they take it into another room to destroy it.

Revoking your will by implication
If you make a later will or codicil containing no revocation clause but containing provisions which are inconsistent with your earlier will, the provisions of your earlier will which are inconsistent with the later one will be considered to be revoked, but the other provisions of the earlier will will remain valid, as will all the provisions of the later will.

If you make a later will or codicil containing no revocation clause and the provisions are not inconsistent with your earlier will, both the earlier will and the later document will be effective.

Revoking your will by an express revocation
By far the best way of revoking provisions of your will is to make a new will or codicil which contains a clause which expressly revokes the earlier will in its entirety or expressly revokes only the provisions which you wish to revoke. If you have several wills, for example a will dealing with your property in England and another will dealing with property abroad, take great care to ensure that the revocation clause revokes only the will that you intend to revoke and that you do not unintentionally revoke both wills. Although section 20 of the Administration of Justice Act 1982

permits a court to rectify a will in cases of clerical error or when a draftsman had failed to understand the testator's instructions and the court has an inherent jurisdiction to omit words from a will when it is proved, if there is an express clause revoking a previous will, there is a strong presumption that it expressed the testator's wishes and clear evidence to the contrary will be required to discharge the very heavy burden of proof which is upon those seeking to contend otherwise.

Dependent relative revocation

For the sake of completeness I mention that if you purport to revoke a will or a bequest on the basis that a new will or bequest which you make is valid, or that the old bequest is covered by the laws of intestacy and this is not so, then the old will or bequest will stand and not be revoked. This rule is known in law as the doctrine of dependent relative revocation. An example is the case of *Re Finnemore (Deceased)* in which the testatrix had made three wills each of which contained revocation clauses and benefited her daughter. The daughter's husband witnessed the last two wills and this would normally cause the bequests to the daughter to fail. However, the court decided that the revocation clauses in the later wills were intended to be conditional upon the gifts to the daughter in those wills taking effect and because the gifts in those wills were made void by the husband witnessing the wills, the bequest to the daughter in the first will would not be revoked and would take effect.

(11)

General Advice Concerning Wills and Associated Matters

KEEPING YOUR WILL SAFE

Your will will be of no use whatsoever if it cannot be found after your death, so make sure that it is kept safely and that your family and your executors know where it is kept. You can also register the whereabouts of your will on the internet website www.lst.locate.co.uk There is no charge for this service which merely notes that you have made a will and where it is to be found. It does not note what the contents of the will are.

If the will is made by a solicitor, he will usually be prepared to keep it in safe custody for you and supply you with a copy free of charge, in the hope that your executors will entrust him with the probate work at the relevant time. Your bank will also be prepared to keep your will in safe custody, but will almost certainly charge an annual fee. If you wish you can deposit your will with the Probate Registry during your lifetime for safe custody at a nominal charge. The fee at the time of writing is £15 and the cheque for the fee should be made payable to HMCS. For details of the procedure and the special envelope in which the documents must be deposited, telephone the Record Keeper's Department of The Principal Probate Registry (020 7947 6948) or write to the department at Principal Probate Registry, 1st Avenue House, 42–49 High Holborn, London WC1V 6NP. The documents are deposited in a sealed envelope and can be deposited in person by you or by someone on your behalf with your authority, at any probate registry or sent by post for deposit to the above address only. If your will is deposited with the Registry it will give you a certificate of deposit which you must keep safely because the certificate will have to be produced if your will is to be produced or withdrawn. There is no fee payable if you wish to withdraw your will from deposit. Depositing your will with the Registry ensures that unscrupulous persons cannot tamper with it after your death. The Registry keeps an index of wills which is searched every time anyone seeks to take out a grant of representation to an estate and thus ensures that your will will not be overlooked and that no earlier will which you may have made, but not destroyed, is proved by mistake. A further possibility is to keep your will in a safe place at home with your other business papers, but if possible make sure it is kept in a fireproof place. Wherever your will is kept it is a good idea to make sure that there is a copy of the will in existence and the copy is kept elsewhere and clearly marked 'copy', because it is sometimes possible to prove a copy will if the original is accidentally destroyed or lost.

To prove your will if it has been lost there must be reasonable evidence both that the will was properly made and what its contents were. As Lord Justice Jacobs said in the case of *Parks v Clout in 2003*, the formalities set out in the Wills Act 'do really matter. One must have a reasonably firm basis for concluding that the formalities were carried out, not merely what the substance of the will was.' Hearsay evidence is admissable to prove the existence or otherwise of the will and the existence and contents of a will can be proved by circumstantial evidence, but there must still be reasonable evidence of both the existence of the will and what its contents were. It must be proved on a balance of probabilities that the will, in those terms, was completed in accordance with the formal requirements of the Wills Act and the burden of proof is upon the person who seeks to uphold the document as a valid will. A higher standard of proof is required to prove fraudulent behaviour such as fraudulent destruction of your will.

Your will or the copy should always be easily accessible to you to refresh your memory on the occasions when you may wish to consider revising it, although you may not wish to consider revising it as frequently as a former Lord Chancellor, Lord St Leonards. He made eight codicils to his will and made his daughter read it through to him so frequently that when the will could not be found after his death, she was able to satisfy a court that she could recite it verbatim!

INFORMATION FOR YOUR EXECUTORS

To assist those you leave behind, create a file or computer disk of the information your executors and family are likely to need at your death and when dealing with your will and winding up your estate. Your family and executors will need to register your death, prove your will and administer your estate and you will not be around to supply information or to tell them where documents can be found! Do not forget to make them aware of the existence of the file and where you keep it.

The file should include the following:

◆ A detailed note of any special funeral wishes. These could include your choice of a preferred funeral director and your request as to the disposal and treatment of the body or of the ashes if there is to be a cremation. A preference could be expressed for a religious or humanist funeral, for special readings or music, for flowers or donations to favoured charities in lieu. Alternatively you could leave these matters to the family's discretion. Give details of any prepaid funeral plans and the deeds of burial rights you may have for a grave.

◆ A notification list of the names, addresses and contact details of all those you wish to be notified of your death.

◆ A note of the whereabouts of your will, birth, civil partnership and marriage certificates, national insurance number, any decree of dissolution of marriage or partnership, pension documents, benefits books or papers. The information in these documents will be required to register your death.

◆ Prepare an assets and liabilities schedule and documents locator to assist your executors when they come to prove your will and settle up your financial affairs. This should include a list of your assets such as bank and building society accounts, National Savings investments, shareholdings and life assurance policies and details of any debts such as personal loans and mortgages. Remember to include a note of where relevant documents such as motor vehicle documents, share or stock certificates, building society pass books, property title deeds, insurance policies documents (including house, contents, life and motor policies), hire, hire-purchase, credit sale and rental agreements can be found and contact details including account numbers (but not security numbers) and addresses. Include your income tax details and details of pensions, credit and debit cards, particulars of any guarantees of any mortgages or other debts you have given, the names and addresses of your accountants and solicitors, the dates and amounts of any gifts you have made which are not exempt from inheritance tax and the identity and current addresses of the beneficiaries.

LIVING WILLS AND ADVANCE DECISIONS

The nature of living wills

Your will is a document which declares your intention as to what shall take place on or after your death and usually, but not necessarily, deals with the disposal of your property. A living will is not a will in the true sense of the word. A living will is the popular name for what lawyers call an advance decision or an advance directive, that is to say, a statement, either written or oral, which sets out what medical treatment you wish, or do not wish, to undergo in specified circumstances before your death. Advance directives are useful in that they will be considered, if at a future date, you lose the power of making decisions or communication, e.g. as a result of falling into a coma or suffering a stroke. They can save your relatives and doctors much worry about what you would wish when agonising decisions have to be made and help them to achieve the correct decision.

Advance directives are recognised by the Common Law and they have received statutory backing in the form of the Mental Capacity Act 2005 as far as they relate to *refusal* of medical treatment.

Differentiating between treatment and nursing care

Medical treatment must not be confused with basic nursing care. There is no right to refuse basic nursing care essential to keep you as comfortable as possible, such as washing and feeding by spoon, as opposed to artificial feeding. Neither can advance decisions be used to prevent you being taken into a care home because that is care and not treatment.

Your best interests

If you make an advance decision that you wish to have a specified medical treatment, your wishes will be taken into account but you cannot insist upon specified treatment because those caring for you are under an obligation to do what is in your best interests. It is for your doctor to make an informed decision in accordance with a responsible and competent body of relevant professional opinion as to what is in your best interests. This can include innovative treatment not previously tried on human beings if there is evidence from responsible medical opinion that does not reject the treatment. He must ask what can be done for you to improve your lot and weigh in the balance the advantages and the disadvantages of any proposed treatment. There is a very strong legal presumption that it is in your best interest to preserve your life but in this context the law does not consider that the prolongation of life is sacrosanct. Other factors such as your wishes, dignity, mental, physical and spiritual welfare and how tolerable the prolongation of your life will be are all factors to be weighed in the balance. These factors are only examples and not exclusive. In the case of *A NHS Trust v B, Holman* J. said that best interests include 'every kind of consideration impacting upon the decision' including 'non-exhaustively medical, emotional, sensory (pleasure, pain and suffering) and instinctive (the human instinct to survive) considerations'.

If there is any doubt the doctor should seek advice from a court.

A right to die?

To have a right to forgo medical treatment or have it withdrawn at your request is not the same thing as having a right to die, even if death will inevitably follow. The European Court has confirmed in the case of *Pretty v The United Kingdom* that there is no general right to die as such in English law. If you are mentally competent but physically incapable, a general right to die would involve the assistance of others in the withdrawal of basic medical care treatment or the introduction of a positive element with the primary intention of causing death, both of which are unlawful euthanasia.

Making a living will under the Common Law

Common Law principles suggest that to be valid your living will must state your true wishes, be made voluntarily, without pressure, influence or encouragement by any other person. Your judgement must not be adversely affected by illness, mental upset or anything else when you make the will. The advance directive should clearly state the nature of the treatment you wish to have or to refuse and the circumstances in which it is to be acted upon. The directive should make it clear that you understand both the treatment and its likely effect. The will must not have been revoked, even orally, by the time the question of carrying out the treatment arises. If tested in a court, even if you are under the age of 18, the court will take into account, but not necessarily follow, your orally expressed wishes. To assist from an evidential point of view if it comes to be tested in court, an advanced directive should be (and in the case of treatment which is necessary to sustain your life must be) made in writing, dated and signed and witnessed in your presence by at least one independent witness who will have nothing to gain from your death. If a doubt or dispute arises concerning your living will treatment will be given to preserve your life and to prevent any deterioration of your condition whilst the problem is resolved.

Making an advance decision after the Mental Capacity Act 2005

The scope of the Act
The Mental Capacity Act 2005 (which in the cause of brevity I shall refer to as 'the Act') contains statutory provisions relating to living wills which it calls advance decisions. The Act seeks to codify and clarify the law relating to decisions to refuse medical treatment made by those who are no longer able to make and communicate their wishes when they were mentally and physically competent to do so. It only deals with decisions to *refuse* treatment and the Common Law as to living wills applies to the extent that it has not been modified by the Act. The Act does not deal with decisions made by those who have mental capacity and are able to make and communicate their wishes at the time of the proposed treatment (including those who at some time previously lost their capacity but have now regained it).

Your mental capacity and ability to make decisions
To make an advance decision under the Act you must be at least 18 years old and you must have the requisite mental capacity to make that particular decision at the time it is made. Your mental capacity is judged according to the decision contemplated and not according to matters generally.

You are assumed to have mental capacity unless the contrary is established on the balance of probabilities. The mere fact that you make a decision which does not seem to be a wise one will not be taken to show that you lack mental capacity. Neither can your incapacity be established merely on the grounds of any condition which you have or any aspect of your behaviour which might lead others to unjustified assumptions. Your age or appearance alone cannot be taken to establish a lack of mental capacity. The test for mental capacity is set out in Section 2(1) of the Act: 'a person lacks capacity in relation to a matter if at the material time he is unable to make a decision for himself in relation to the matter because of an impairment of, or a disturbance in the functioning of, the mind or brain'.

According to Section 3 (1) of the Act a person is considered unable to make a decision if he is unable:

a) 'to understand the information relevant to the decision,
b) to retain that information,
c) to use or weigh that information as part of the process of making the decision; or
d) to communicate his decision (whether by talking, using sign language or any other means).'

Section 3(4) provides that:

'The information relevant to a decision includes information about the reasonably foreseeable consequences of:

(a) deciding one way or another; or
(b) failing to make the decision.'

The form of a valid advance decision
The person proposing to carry out treatment must accept an

advance decision as to refusal of treatment if the decision is validly made and is applicable to the relevant treatment. It is therefore essential that your advance decision clearly specifies the treatment that you wish to avoid and the circumstances in which it is not to be given or continued but you may specify them in lay terms if you do so unambiguously. However, you would be well advised to discuss your decision with your doctor before you lose capacity and to ask him to record the discussion in your medical notes to ensure that your specification of the treatment and the relevant circumstances are sufficiently precise and to provide evidence that you were fully aware of the nature of the treatment and the consequences of refusing it.

If the decision upon which you intend to rely is only expressed orally and it can be adequately proved, it will be valid unless it involves a refusal of life-sustaining treatment. A refusal of life-sustaining treatment must contain a statement by you to the effect that it is to apply to that treatment even if your life is put at risk by the refusal and must be made in writing and be signed by you or by someone on your behalf and witnessed. Your signature and that of the witness must be made or acknowledged in the presence of each other. Section 4(10) of the Act defines life-sustaining treatment as 'treatment that in the view of the person providing health care for the person concerned is necessary to sustain life'.

Revoking your advance decision
Your advance decision will cease to be valid if, when you have the mental capacity to do so:

* you expressly withdraw it; or

- you do something which by implication shows that you intend to withdraw it or that it is no longer your fixed decision; or

- you *later* make a Lasting Power of Attorney which gives someone the power to consent to or to refuse the treatment to which the advance decision relates; or

- there are reasonable grounds for believing that circumstances exist which you did not anticipate at the time you made the advance decision and if you had anticipated them you would not have made it. Such circumstances might be new methods of treatment or the production of new drugs.

The case of *HE v A Hospital NHS Trust*, which was decided before the Act, is an example of example of conduct, which by implication, showed an intention to withdraw an advance decision. In that case betrothal to a Muslim was held to revoke an advance directive which refused treatment involving blood products, the directive having been made by a lady when she was a practising Jehovah's Witness.

You may withdraw or amend an advance decision if you have the capacity to do so and the withdrawal or amendment does not have to be made in writing unless the alteration results in a decision to refuse life-sustaining treatment, in which case it must follow the formalities for making such a decision.

If you make an advance decision you should review it frequently because your wishes may change in the light of advances in medical science and care should be taken to ensure that you make the existence of the decision and any changes to it known to your doctor, e.g. by lodging it with him. Discussing the will with the family members could lead to the suggestion that they may have applied undue influence.

ENDURING AND LASTING POWERS OF ATTORNEY

In the same way as your will makes provision for your wishes to be carried out when you are no longer alive, a Lasting Power of Attorney is a useful tool to appoint someone you trust and have confidence in to act for you if you become incapable of acting for yourself during your lifetime. With average life expectancy increasing such situations are arising more frequently. Most lawyers consider that it is almost as important for you to set up a Lasting Power of Attorney as it is to make a will and that wills and Lasting Powers of Attorney complement each other.

A Power of Attorney is a document by which a person (the donor) gives to one or more people he or she chooses (the attorney(s)) power to deal with some specified welfare matters or financial affairs and property of the donor, or the donor's welfare matters and property generally. Powers of Attorney differ from Living Wills in that Living Wills are confined to medical treatment but Powers of Attorney can relate to matters generally.

Before 1985, Powers of Attorney automatically became ineffective if you became mentally incapable and it was necessary for an application to be made to the then Court of Protection to appoint a Receiver to manage your financial matters for you under the court's supervision. Receivership applications were onerous, lengthy and very expensive. In 1985 Parliament passed the Enduring Powers of Attorney Act which created a new, simple form of power of attorney called an Enduring Power of Attorney that survives any mental incapacity you suffer, provided that (a) you were over the age of 18 and mentally capable when you signed it, (b) you were not an undischarged bankrupt, (c) you used the prescribed form of document and (d) that you followed the procedures set up by the Act.

The Mental Capacity Act 2005 repealed the Enduring Powers of Attorney Act 1985, but Enduring Powers of Attorney in existence when it came into force on the first of October 2007 continue to have the same legal effect that they had at that time and are governed by the rules and procedures then in force. From that date, a new form of power of attorney called a Lasting Power of Attorney created by the Mental Capacity Act 2005 to fill the gap left by the repeal of the Enduring Powers of Attorney Act 1985 must be used if a new power of attorney is to survive the incapacity of its maker.

Lasting Powers of Attorney
There are two types of Lasting Powers of Attorney.

1. Personal Health Care and Welfare Lasting Powers of Attorney which can be used to make health or welfare decisions such as where the donor will live and which come into force when they have been registered with the Public Guardian and the donor of the Power is no longer capable.

2. Property and Financial Affairs Lasting Powers of Attorney which come into force and can be used when they have been registered, whether or not the donor of the Power is still capable, unless they contain a restriction to the contrary.

The principal difference between Enduring Powers of Attorney and Lasting Powers of Attorney is that the scope of Lasting Powers of Attorney is wider in that they can deal with personal healthcare decisions and welfare and are not confined to financial matters.

What you can do and what you cannot do by giving a Lasting Power of Attorney
Your attorney must register the Lasting Power of Attorney with the Office of the Public Guardian before he can exercise the powers given to him. When the Power of Attorney is in force, unless it places limits on his powers, your attorney can do almost anything you could have done, for example the attorney can sell your shares or other property, use your bank account and make gifts of a reasonable amount from your assets proportionate to your wealth on birthdays, wedding anniversaries, Christmas and other customary occasions to those connected with you (even to the attorney), or to charities which you might reasonably be expected to support.

Your attorney cannot be appointed to act in matters of personal status such as consenting to adoption, marriage, civil partnership, divorce or matters under the Human Fertilisation and Embryology Act 1990. He cannot make a decision discharging parental responsibilities in matters not relating to a child's property. Lasting Powers of Attorney cannot be used to give or refuse consent to life-sustaining treatment unless the Power contains an express provision to that effect. Your attorney cannot be given power to vote for you or to appoint anyone to act in his stead or as his successor. Neither can he make a will for you, but he can ask The Court of Protection to make a will for you if that is in your interest.

If you wish to delegate powers which you have as a trustee, a solicitor should be consulted because the law concerning a trustee's power to delegate is complex.

It is possible to limit your attorney's powers by inserting restrictions, for example the Power can state that it is not to come into effect until you become incapable, that it is to be limited to managing investments, that all cheques over a specified sum require two signatures, or that certain specified transactions, such as the sale of a property, cannot take place without the consent of your spouse or all of your children.

Although you can create a Lasting Power of Attorney which is limited to come into effect only after you have become mentally incapable, the Lasting Power of Attorney must be completed while you have the mental capacity to make it.

The mental capacity you need to make a Lasting Power of Attorney
The mental capacity you need to make a Lasting Power of Attorney is the same as that you need to make an advance decision (see page 190).

Choosing and appointing an attorney for your Lasting Power of Attorney
Because the attorney is often given very wide powers, the choice of attorney is very important. Your attorney should be a compassionate person who can be trusted to act in your interests. The relevant factors to be borne in mind in the choice of an executor are relevant to the choice of an attorney. (Please refer to Chapter 4.)

Some solicitors, accountants and trust companies will act as attorneys, but they will wish to charge and you might consider that it is cumbersome and expensive to employ professionals to do tasks that can be done by a layman, such as shopping or clearing your home if it is necessary for you to move into residential care. You can have separate powers of attorney to appoint different attorneys to act for you in different matters but to do so they must be very carefully drafted to avoid overlap and confusion. A trust corporation can only act as your attorney in relation to your property and your affairs and not in relation to your health or welfare.

If you appoint a person as your attorney he must be at least 18 years old, mentally capable and, if he is to be an attorney in respect of your property and affairs, he must not be bankrupt.

If more than one person is appointed attorney they may be appointed to act jointly, in which case one cannot act without the other and if one refuses the appointment, dies, or becomes bankrupt or otherwise incapable of acting the Power will become ineffective. Alternatively the attorneys may be appointed to act jointly and severally, in which case each has power to act alone and the Power remains effective as long as there is one attorney who is capable of acting and willing to act. If you do not specify whether they are appointed jointly or jointly and severally it is taken that they are appointed to act jointly.

You cannot give your attorney power to appoint a successor or substitute but you can provide in the Power who shall succeed him if the appointment is terminated because he disclaims the appointment, dies, becomes bankrupt, loses his capacity to act as an attorney or he is your spouse or civil partner and the marriage or partnership is dissolved or annulled.

If both you and your spouse or partner wish to make Lasting Powers of Attorney, you must both make separate Lasting Powers of Attorney because, although a person can appoint several attorneys or make several Lasting Powers of Attorney to run concurrently in respect of different assets or matters with different attorneys and several people can appoint the same attorneys, several people cannot make a joint Lasting Power of Attorney.

The form of your Lasting Power of Attorney
Your Lasting Power of Attorney must be in the form prescribed by the Act and The Lasting Powers of Attorney and Public Guardian Regulations 2007 (Statutory Instrument Number 1253) made under the Act and must be registered with the Public Guardian. If it is not, it will be invalid and not give any power to the person you wish to appoint as your attorney unless the Public Guardian agrees to waive a minor defect in it or the Court of Protection can be persuaded that when you made it you believed you were making a Lasting Power of Attorney.

The prescribed form contains a certificate by a person who fulfils one of several descriptions contained in the regulations made under the Act to the effect that:

- you understand the purpose of the Lasting Power of Attorney which is made without undue influence or pressure and the scope of the authority it gives to your attorney; and

- there is nothing which would prevent it from creating a Lasting Power of Attorney.

Registering your Lasting Power of Attorney
Your Lasting Power of Attorney is of no effect until it has been

registered with the Public Guardian and you can name up to five people the Office of the Public Guardian must notify and give an opportunity to object before registering the Power. If an objection is received and sustained the Power will not be registered. The Court of Protection can remove a non-compliant provision from a Power and if it then complies with the requirements for a valid Lasting Power of Attorney and there is no other objection which is sustained, it will be registered but a note of the amendment will be attached to the Power.

The prescribed forms to create and register a Lasting Power of Attorney can be obtained from the Office of the Public Guardian, POBox 15118, Birmingham B16 6GX, telephone: 0845 330 2900, fax: 020 7664 7551, email: *customerservices@publicguardian.gsi. gov.uk*. The forms can be downloaded from the Office of the Public Guardian's website (*www.publicguardian.gsi. gov.uk*) and are also available from a law stationer such as Hammicks or Solicitors Law Stationery Company. The current fee for registering a Lasting Power of Attorney is £120. Official copies of a registered Lasting or Enduring Power of Attorney can be obtained from the Office of the Public Guardian for a fee of £25.

Revoking your Lasting Power of Attorney
You may revoke a Lasting Power of Attorney if you have mental capacity and your Lasting Power of Attorney will also be revoked

◆ As far as it relates to your property and affairs, if you become bankrupt, but the making of an interim bankruptcy restrictions order against you does not revoke the Power; it merely suspends it until the order no longer has effect.

♦ If your attorney disclaims the appointment, dies, or loses his capacity to act as an attorney, unless it provides for a substitute attorney or he is one of several joint and several attorneys and after the event at least one of the attorneys remains.

♦ If your attorney becomes bankrupt, the bankruptcy will terminate his powers as far as they relate to your property and affairs and unless the Lasting Power of Attorney provides for a substitute attorney or he is one of several joint and several attorneys and when he becomes bankrupt at least one of the attorneys remains, the Power of Attorney will be revoked thus far. The making of an interim bankruptcy restrictions order against your attorney merely suspends his powers in relation to your property and affairs until the order no longer has effect. Your attorney's bankruptcy does not revoke the attorney's powers or revoke the Power as far as they relate to your personal welfare.

♦ If your attorney is your spouse or civil partner and the marriage or partnership is dissolved or annulled, his powers will be terminated and the Power of Attorney revoked unless it states that this shall not be so.

The statutory Code of Practice
Your attorney empowered by a Lasting Power of Attorney is under a legal obligation to act in your best interests at all times and in accordance with a lengthy Code of Practice provided by the Mental Capacity Act 2005 and which can be seen on the Office of the Public Guardian website at *wwwguardianship.gov.uk*.

PERIODIC REVIEWS AND DEEDS OF FAMILY ARRANGEMENT

Finally do not forget to review your finances and the provisions of your will periodically to check whether your will is still appropriate having regard to changes in

- tax rules;
- tax rates;
- your wealth and the value of your various assets;
- your family and the coming of age of your children;
- your or your beneficiaries' marriages, civil partnerships, divorces and the making and ending of friendships.

If your will is not appropriate to your family circumstances and not tax-efficient at the time of your death, it is sometimes possible for your beneficiaries to change the will to make it more appropriate to all concerned by entering into a document called a deed of family arrangement within two years of your death. If one of your beneficiaries has died after your death, provided they have the consent of those who benefit under his will or intestacy, his personal representatives can also disclaim or vary his inheritance by entering into such a deed.

If an asset has been redirected once to a different beneficiary by a deed of variation, it is not permissible to redirect it a second time, but more than one deed of variation can be entered into in respect of an estate as long as they relate to different assets.

Do not rely upon your beneficiaries or their personal representatives entering into a deed of family arrangement; they may be reluctant to change what they believe to be your last wishes and it might not be possible to do so. Any such deed will require the consent of all concerned. If minors or others without full legal capacity are involved, an application to a court to approve the arrangement on their behalf will have to be made and the court will only give its approval if it considers that the arrangement is to the benefit of the person who lacks capacity. Moreover the court proceedings might make the time limit impossible to comply with and court proceedings are expensive.

If the deed is to be effective for tax purposes it must contain a statement to the effect that the Inheritance Tax Act 1984 shall apply as if any variation had been made by you or, as the case may be, any disclaimed benefit had not been conferred by your will and your executors must be a party to the declaration if the effect of the deed is to increase the amount of tax payable. The executors can only refuse to be a party to the declaration if no or insufficient assets are held by them in their capacity as executors to pay the additional tax. If the effect of the deed is to increase the amount of tax payable a copy of it must also be sent to HMRC within six months of the date of the document, together with a statement of the additional tax payable, or there will be the possibility that HMRC will levy a fine.

In the case of any estate where the residue is either partially or wholly exempt from inheritance tax, it will be necessary to carefully consider whether any proposed disclaimer or variation will cause the total value of the non-exempt gifts to exceed the nil rate band as a result of the grossing up rules which are explained in Chapter 6, page 137.

Deeds of family arrangement can also be used to vary inheritance rights which arise on intestacy and in spite of their name, need not be by deed as long as they are made in writing.

The formalities for tax effective deeds of family arrangements have to be strictly observed. Such matters require professional assistance and are not cheap. Moreover it is always open to the government of the day to amend the law as to deeds of arrangement. It is much better to review your will regularly and to get and keep it right than to rely upon the possibility of variation after death.

Appendix:
Specimen Forms and Documents

SPECIMEN FORM OF NOTICE OF SEVERANCE OF JOINT TENANCY

From (*insert your full names and your address*)

To (*insert name(s) and address(es) of the other joint owners*)

Re (*insert the address or a description of the property*)

I HEREBY GIVE YOU NOTICE that I (*insert your name and address*) hereby sever the joint tenancy which exists between us in the above property so that in future we shall hold it as beneficial tenants in common AND I REQUEST that you acknowledge that you have received this notice by signing and returning the enclosed copy notice to me.

Dated (*insert date*)

Signed (*insert your signature*)

Note: A notice in these terms should be given to each joint owner. The following should be written or typed as appropriate on each copy notice on the next line following your signature:

'Received a notice of which the above is a copy this   day of   two thousand and

SIGNED_____

SPECIMEN NOTE AS TO REASONS WHY A POTENTIAL CLAIMANT UNDER THE INHERITANCE (PROVISION FOR FAMILY AND DEPENDANTS) ACT 1975 HAS BEEN LEFT NO OR ONLY A LIMITED INHERITANCE

To my Executors.

I (*insert your full names*) of (*insert your address*) hereby declare that I have made (*insert 'no' or 'no further' as appropriate*) provision for (*insert relationship, if any, and name of the person concerned*) in my will of this date because (*state reason or reasons, e.g.*

I have made alternative provision for him in my lifetime.

or

I consider that I have fulfilled my obligations to him in my lifetime.

or

I consider that I should devote the majority of my estate to (*insert relationship and name of the person concerned*) whom I consider to be less wealthy and in greater need.

or

I consider that I should devote the majority of my estate to (*insert relationship and name of the person concerned*) who has borne the major part of the responsibility for caring for me in my declining years.

or

(*insert relationship, if any, and name of the person concerned*) has cut himself off from me and I have neither seen or heard from him for (*insert number*) years.

Dated this (*insert date*)

Signed (*insert your signature*).

Note: This document and the will should both be signed and dated with the same date.

MUTUAL WILLS AGREEMENT AND DECLARATION

(insert name of other party concerned) and I agree and declare that our respective wills dated *(insert the date)* are/are not mutual wills and that each of us is/is not free to dispose of or materially adversely affect the value of (insert 'the assets of our respective estates' or *a description of the relevant bequest*) in any way he or she thinks fit in the future.

Note: If the wills are to be mutual wills add the following:

We further declare that if and whenever either of us remarries he or she shall before the remarriage make a will stated to be made in contemplation of the marriage and which will shall contain a declaration to give effect to the restriction contained in the preceding declaration.

Note: The agreement should be signed by both parties, dated and made in duplicate. Each party should keep one signed copy and the agreement can either be produced as a separate document or written at the end of the will after the signatures of the witnesses to the will.

BASIC SKELETON FORM OF A WILL FOR THE RESIDUARY BENEFICIARIES TO BENEFIT EQUALLY

THIS IS THE LAST WILL of me *(insert your full names, address and occupation, if any)* ⸻

1.   I REVOKE all wills and testamentary dispositions previously made by me⸻

2.   I APPOINT *(insert full names, addresses and occupations of proposed executors)* to be the executors of this my will, but if neither of them survive me or having survived me both of them shall be unwilling or unable to accept the office of executor or for any other reason the appointment fails to take effect then I APPOINT *(insert full names, addresses and occupations of proposed alternative executors)* to be the executors of my will⸻

3(a)   I APPOINT the person or people who take out the first grant of representation to be obtained in respect of my estate to be the trustees of my estate⸻

(b)   THE expression 'my trustees' wherever used in this my will shall mean the trustees or trustee for the time being whether original, substituted or added⸻

4. I GIVE

(a)   the sum of (*insert the amount in words and in figures*) to (*each of*) the said (*insert the full names of the relevant executor or executors*) absolutely if (s)he shall prove my will_____

(b)   the sum of (*insert the amount in words and in figures*) to (*insert full names and address of the legatee*)_____

These legacies are in addition to any other benefit the legatee(s) may receive from my estate_____

5.   I BEQUEATH

(a)   my (*insert a sufficient description of the article given to enable it to be identified and distinguished from any other of your possessions*) to (*insert full names and address of proposed beneficiary*)___

(b)   any (*insert a sufficient description of the article given to enable it to be identified and distinguished from any other of your possessions*) which I shall own at the date of my death to (*insert full names and address of proposed beneficiary*)_____

6.   I GIVE DEVISE BEQUEATH AND APPOINT all my estate not otherwise disposed of by my will or by any codicil to my will to my trustees UPON TRUST to use it to pay my debts, funeral and testamentary expenses and the legacies bequeathed by my will or by any codicil to my will and all tax and other fiscal impositions payable on or in respect of my estate or any part thereof as a result of my death and to hold what remains for such of (*insert the full names and addresses of the proposed beneficiaries*) as shall be living at the date of my death and if more than one for them for them equally BUT IF any of them shall die before me and shall leave a child or children who survive me such child or children shall inherit and if more than one equally between them the share of my estate which his or her parent would have inherited had he or she survived me_____

7.   I DECLARE that

(a)   no potential beneficiary under this my will shall take any interest thereby unless he she or it shall survive me by one calendar month (*if required insert 'and attain the age of' and a chosen age 'either before or after my death but within twenty one years of my death'*)

(b)   when quantifying the entitlement of any beneficiary on my death no account shall be taken of any gifts made by me in my lifetime

(c)   my trustees may in their sole discretion and without requiring the consent of any other person appropriate at such valuation as they shall reasonably decide any assets of my estate in or towards the satisfaction of any testamentary bequest made by me_____

(d)   the receipt of the person who seems to my trustees to be the treasurer or other proper officer of any organisation or the parent or guardian of any minor who is a beneficiary under the terms of my will shall be a sufficient discharge to my trustees for any bequest and that my trustees shall not be obliged to check how the bequest is used

(e)   unless they have acted with gross negligence or in bad faith in carrying out or delaying the carrying out of or failing to carry out their duties in relation to my will my trustees shall not be held responsible for any losses suffered by the beneficiaries of my estate_____

8.   IF my trustees shall not be aware of the whereabouts of any beneficiary under the terms of my will after having complied with section 27 of the Trustee Act 1925 my trustees may distribute my estate on the basis that such beneficiary has died before me or ceased to exist before my death_____

9.   I EXPRESS the wish that after my death my body shall be buried and not cremated_____

I N   W I T N E S S whereof I have signed this my will the   day of   Two thousand and   _____

SIGNED by the before named
(*insert your full names*) in our joint } Testator to sign here
presence and then by us in his

First witness to sign here

and print his name here

and write his address and occupation, if any, here.

Second witness to sign here

and print his name here

and write his address and occupation, if any, here.

Notes

1. It is not necessary to leave a legacy as provided in clause 4(a).

2. The legacies given in clauses 4 and 5 of the above will have been given free of inheritance tax so that any tax payable will be paid out of the remainder of the estate and borne by the beneficiaries named in clause 6. If it is intended that any of the bequests should bear their own share of inheritance tax insert the words 'subject to inheritance tax' after the description of the relevant bequest and 'except where otherwise stated above' in clause 6 after the words 'as a result of my death'. In deciding whether gifts should bear their proportion of inheritance tax please consider the possible grossing up of gifts discussed in Chapter 6.

3. If clause 4 is omitted from the will the words 'by my will or' should be omitted where they appear for a second time in clause 6.

4. The words from and including 'BUT IF' to the end of clause 6 should be omitted if it is not intended that children of predeceasing parents should inherit their parents' share.

5. If clause 7(a) is used and the beneficiary's entitlement is made dependent upon reaching a specified age, the words 'within twenty one years of my death' must be included to avoid the risk of the bequest being void as infringing the perpetuity rule.

6. If a beneficiary's entitlement is made dependent upon reaching a specified age consider including the following sub-clause as 7(f) 'My trustees shall have power in their sole discretion to use for the benefit of any potential beneficiary part or the entirety of the income and capital of my estate to which the beneficiary may become entitled.'

7. If any of the people named in your will are related to you their identity can be further clarified by inserting the relationship.

ALTERNATIVE PROVISION TO BE USED IN THE SKELETON FORM OF A WILL IF YOU WISH TO LEAVE THE ESTATE TO YOUR SPOUSE OR CIVIL PARTNER FOR LIFE OR UNTIL SHE REMARRIES AND AFTERWARDS TO OTHER BENEFICIARIES

Instead of clause 6 insert the following clause:

6.   I GIVE DEVISE BEQUEATH AND APPOINT all my estate not otherwise disposed of by my will or by any codicil to my will to my trustees UPON TRUST to use it to pay my debts funeral and testamentary expenses and the legacies bequeathed by my will or by any codicil and all tax and other fiscal impositions payable in respect of my estate or any part of my estate as a result of my death and to invest what remains and pay the net income produced by the investments to my (*insert 'husband', 'wife' or 'civil partner' as appropriate and your spouse's or civil partner's full names*) until (*insert 'he' or 'she' as appropriate*) remarries, enters into a civil partnership or dies and afterwards to hold the investments and the income they produce for such of (*insert full names and addresses of proposed beneficiaries*) as shall be living at that date and if more than one for them equally BUT IF any of them shall have died before then and shall leave a child or children who are then living such child or children shall inherit and if more than one equally between them the share of my estate which his or her parent would have inherited if he or she not so died._____

Notes

1. This clause can be adapted for use if you wish to give a life interest to a beneficiary who is not your spouse or civil partner but before deciding to leave only a life or other limited interest in your estate, bear in mind what I have written in Chapters 3 and 6 about impoverishing your spouse or civil partner and about the Inheritance (Provision for Family and Dependants) Act 1975.

2. Do not attempt to leave successive life or other limited interests without taking professional advice or you may well fall foul of the rules against perpetuities.

3. If you decide to leave a life or other limited interest in your estate you should consider including the following additional clauses:

'( )   MY TRUSTEES shall have power to invest the assets of my estate and vary investments in all respects as if they were their own and to borrow upon the security of such assets upon such terms and for such purposes as they think fit_____

( )   MY TRUSTEES shall have power to retain or purchase freehold or leasehold property as an authorised investment and to permit it to be used as a residence for one or more beneficiaries or potential benefici-aries (including life tenants) of the residue of my estate upon such terms as to repair decoration maintenance alterations improvement insurance heating lighting payment of electricity and gas charges water rates sewage charges Council Tax and other outgoings as my trustees shall think fit_____

( ) THE FOLLOWING statutory provisions shall not apply to my will or to any codicil hereto: sections 11 (1) and 19 of The Trusts of Land and Appointment of Trustees Act 1996_____

( )   MY TRUSTEES shall have power in their sole discretion to use part or the entirety of the income and capital of my estate to which a beneficiary may become entitled for the benefit of the beneficiary

( )   I DECLARE that there shall be no apportionment of the income of my estate to the intent that the Apportionment Act 1870 and the equitable rules of apportionment shall be excluded from the administra-tion of my estate_____

( )   UNLESS they have acted with gross negligence or in bad faith in carrying out or delaying or failing to carry out their duties in relation to my will my trustees shall not be held responsible for any losses suffered by the beneficiaries of my estate_____

( )   My trustees may exercise or refrain from exercising the powers contained in my will notwithstanding that in doing so any of them shall benefit personally provided that they act in good faith_____'

4. If you leave a limited interest, such as a life interest, in your estate to your spouse or civil partner it will avoid possible confusion and disputes as to ownership if you also include the following clause:

'I bequeath my personal chattels as defined by section 55 (1) (x) of the Administration of Estates Act 1925 which are not otherwise bequeathed by my will to my *(insert civil partner, wife or husband as appropriate)*'

ALTERNATIVE PROVISION TO BE USED IN THE SKELETON FORM OF A WILL IF YOU WISH THE RESIDUARY BENEFICIARIES TO BENEFIT UNEQUALLY

Instead of clause 6 insert the following clause:

6.   I GIVE DEVISE BEQUEATH AND APPOINT all my estate not otherwise disposed of by my will or by any codicil to my will to my trustees UPON TRUST to use it to pay my debts funeral and testamentary expenses and the legacies given by my will or by any codicil to the will and all tax and other fiscal impositions payable on or in respect of my estate or any part thereof as a result of my death and to divide what remains into *(insert in words rather than figures the relevant number of shares)* shares and to hold *(insert in words rather than figures the relevant number of shares)* shares for *(insert full names and address of the first proposed beneficiary)* and to hold a further *(insert in words rather than figures the relevant number of shares)* shares for *(insert full names and address of the next proposed beneficiary and continue in this way until all the shares have been disposed of)* BUT IF any of them shall die in my lifetime and leave a child or children who survive me such child or children shall inherit and if more than one equally between them the share of my residuary estate which his or her parent would have inherited if he or she had survived me AND IF any of them shall die in my lifetime and leave no child or children who survive me the share given to him or her shall not lapse but shall accrue and be added proportionately to the other share or shares the trusts of which have not failed and shall be held by my trustees upon the same trusts as such other share or shares——————————————————

Notes

1. If you intended that any of the bequests should bear their own share of inheritance tax insert the words 'subject to inheritance tax' after the description of the relevant bequest and 'except where otherwise stated above' in clause 6 after the words 'as a result of my death'. In deciding whether gifts should bear their proportion

of inheritance tax consider the possible grossing up of gifts discussed in Chapter 6.

2. If you do not intend that the children of any proposed beneficiary who dies before you shall inherit the share which the parent would have inherited delete the words from and including 'BUT IF' to the end of the clause and substitute

'BUT IF any of them shall die in my lifetime the share given to him or her shall not lapse but shall accrue and be added proportionately to the other share or shares the trusts of which have not failed and shall be held by my trustees upon the same trusts as such other share or shares_____'

WILL LEAVING THE ENTIRE ESTATE TO YOUR SPOUSE OR CIVIL PARTNER AND APPOINTING HER AS THE SOLE EXECUTRIX WITH ALTERNATIVE PROVISIONS SHOULD SHE DIE BEFORE YOU

THIS IS THE LAST WILL of me (*insert your full names, address and occupation*)_____

1.   I REVOKE all wills and testamentary dispositions previously made by me_____

2.   IF my (*insert wife, husband or civil partner and the spouse's or civil partner's full names and address*) shall survive me (*if required insert by one calendar month or other suitable period*) I GIVE DEVISE BEQUEATH AND APPOINT all my estate to my said (*insert wife, husband or civil partner, as appropriate*) for (*insert her or his as appropriate*) own use and benefit absolutely and APPOINT (*insert her or him, as appropriate*) to be the sole (*insert executrix if she is female or executor if he is male*) of this my will_____

3.   IF clause 2 of my will shall fail the following clauses of my will shall have effect_____

4.   I APPOINT (*insert full names, addresses and occupations of the first proposed alternative executors*) to be the executors of this my will but if neither of them survive me or having survived me they shall both be

unwilling or unable to accept the office of executor or for ~~reason~~ the appointment fails to take effect then I APPOINT (*i   full names, addresses and occupations of the second proposed alternative executors*) to be the executors of my will_____

5(a)   I APPOINT the person or people who take out the first grant of representation to be obtained in respect of my estate to be the trustees of my estate_____

(b)   THE expression 'my trustees' wherever used in this my will shall mean the trustees or trustee for the time being whether original substituted or added_____

6.   I APPOINT (*insert full names addresses and occupations of proposed guardians*) to be the guardians of those of my children who are minors at the time of my death_____

7.   I GIVE

(a)   the sum of (*insert the amount in words and in figures*) to (*each of*) the said (*insert the full names of the relevant executor or executors*) absolutely if (*insert 'he' or 'she' or 'they' as appropriate*) shall prove my will_____

(b)   the sum of (*insert the amount in words and in figures*) to (*insert full names and address of the legatee*)_____

These legacies are in addition to any other benefit the legatee(s) may receive from my estate_____

8.   I BEQUEATH

(a) my (*insert sufficient description of the article given to enable it to be identified and distinguished from any other of your possessions*) to (*insert full names and address of proposed beneficiary*)___

(b) any (*insert sufficient description of the article given to enable it to be identified and distinguished from any other of your possessions*) which I shall own at the date of my death to (*insert full names and address of proposed beneficiary*)_____

9.   I GIVE DEVISE BEQUEATH AND APPOINT all my estate not otherwise disposed of by my will or by any codicil to my will to my trustees UPON TRUST to pay from it my debts funeral and testamentary expenses and legacies bequeathed by my will or by any codicil to my will and all tax and other fiscal impositions payable on or in respect of my estate or any part thereof as a result of my death and to hold what

remains for such of my children as shall be living at the date of my death and attain the age of (*insert the chosen age not exceeding 21*) either before or after my death and if more than one equally between them BUT IF any of my children shall not survive me and attain that age and shall leave a child or children who survive me such child or children shall take and if more than one equally between them the share of my estate which his or her parent would have taken had he or she survived me and attained that age

10. I DECLARE that

(a)   no potential beneficiary under this my will shall take any interest therein unless he she or it shall survive me by one calendar month (*if required insert 'and attain the age of' and a chosen age 'either before or after my death but within twenty one years of my death'*)

(b)   when quantifying the entitlement of any beneficiary on my death no account shall be taken of any gifts made by me in my lifetime

(c)   my trustees may in their sole discretion and without requiring the consent of any other person appropriate at such valuation as they shall reasonably decide any assets of my estate in or towards the satisfaction of any testamentary bequest made by me_____

(d)   my trustees shall have power to invest the assets of my estate and vary investments in all respects as if they were their own and to borrow upon the security of such assets upon such terms and for such purposes as they think fit_____

(e)   the receipt of the person who seems to my trustees to be the treasurer or other proper officer of any organisation or the parent or guardian of any minor who is a beneficiary under the terms of my will shall be a sufficient discharge to my trustees for the bequest and that my trustees shall not be obliged to check how the bequest is used

(f)   unless they have acted with gross negligence or in bad faith in carrying out or delaying the carrying out of or failing to carry out their duties in relation to my will my trustees shall not be held responsible for any losses suffered by the beneficiaries of my estate____

(g) the following statutory provisions shall not apply to my will or to any codicil to my will: sections 11 (1) and 19 of the Trusts of Land and Appointment of Trustees Act 1990_____

11. IF my trustees shall not be aware of the whereabouts of any beneficiary under the terms of this my will after having complied with section 27 of the Trustee Act 1925 my trustees may distribute my estate on the basis that such beneficiary has predeceased me or ceased to exist before my death_____

12. MY TRUSTEES may exercise or refrain from exercising the powers contained in my will notwithstanding that in doing so any of them shall benefit personally provided that they act in good faith_____

13. MY (*insert wife, husband or civil partner as appropriate*) and I agree that our respective wills are/are not mutual wills and that each of us is/is not free to dispose of his/her property in any way he or she thinks fit in the future_____

14. I EXPRESS the wish that after my death my body shall be buried and not cremated_____

I N W I T N E S S whereof I have signed this my will this   day of   Two thousand and   _____

SIGNED by the before named ⎫
(*insert your full names*) in our joint ⎬ Testator to sign here
presence and then by us in his ⎭

First witness to sign here

and print his name here

and write his address and occupation, if any, here

Second witness to sign here

and print his name here

and write his address and occupation, if any, here

Notes

1. It is not necessary to leave a legacy as provided in clause 7(a).

2. The legacies given in clauses 7 and 8 of the above will have been given free of inheritance tax so that any tax payable will be paid out of the remainder of the estate and borne by the beneficiaries

named in clause 9. If it is intended that any of the bequests should bear their own share of inheritance tax insert the words 'subject to inheritance tax' after the description of the relevant bequest and 'except where otherwise stated above' in clause 9 after the words 'as a result of my death'. In deciding whether gifts should bear their proportion of inheritance tax consider the possible grossing up of gifts discussed in Chapter 6.

3. If clause 8 is omitted from the will the words 'by my will or' where they follow 'not otherwise disposed of' should be omitted from clause 9.

4. The words from and including 'BUT IF' to the end of clause 9 should be omitted if it is not intended that children of predeceasing parents should inherit their parents' share.

5. If clause 10(a) is used and the beneficiary's entitlement is made dependent upon reaching a specified age, the words 'but within twenty one years of my death' must be included to avoid the risk of the bequest being void as infringing the perpetuity rule.

6. If there is any possibility of a beneficiary being under age consider including the following sub-clause as 10(h):

    'My trustees shall have power in their sole discretion to use for the benefit of any beneficiary part or the entirety of the income and capital of my estate to which the beneficiary may become entitled.'

7. If any of the people named in your will are related to you their identity can be further clarified by inserting the relationship.

ADDITIONAL CLAUSES FOR SPECIAL WILLS

Additional clauses to be inserted in a will made with a marriage in mind

THIS WILL is made with my intended marriage to *(insert intended spouse's full names)* in mind and shall not be revoked by the marriage
IF the marriage takes place the following clauses of my will shall have

effect_____
(*insert the relevant required clauses*)

<u>IF</u> the marriage does not take place the following clauses of my will shall have effect_____
(*insert the relevant required clauses*)

Note: The above clauses can be adapted for use in a will which is made with a civil partnership in view.

Consider including some or all of the following clauses additionally to those contained in the skeleton will.

In a will containing gifts to under-age beneficiaries

Appointment of guardians
<u>I APPOINT</u> (*insert full names, addresses and occupations of proposed guardians*) to be the guardians of those of my children who are minors

Advancement clause
<u>MY TRUSTEES</u> shall have power in their sole discretion to use part or the entirety of the income and capital of my estate to which a beneficiary may become entitled for the benefit of the beneficiary

Receipt clause for a bequest
<u>THE RECEIPT</u> of the parent or guardian of any minor who is a beneficiary under the terms of my will shall be a sufficient discharge to my trustees for the bequest and my trustees shall not be obliged to see how the bequest is used_____

Power to invest and borrow
<u>MY TRUSTEES</u> shall have power to invest the assets of my estate and vary investments in all respects as if they were their own and to borrow upon the security of the assets and investments upon such terms and for such purposes as they think fit_____

Exclusion of statutory powers relating to trustees' duty to consult with beneficiaries and beneficiaries' power to appoint and remove trustees

THE FOLLOWING statutory provisions shall not apply to my will or to any codicil to my will: sections 11 (1) and 19 of the Trusts of Land and Appointment of Trustees Act 1996———————————————————

In a will which contains a bequest to an organisation

Receipt clause for a bequest
THE RECEIPT of the person who seems to my trustees to be the treasurer or other proper officer of any organisation which is a beneficiary under the terms of my will shall be a sufficient discharge to my trustees for the bequest and my trustees shall not be obliged to see how the bequest is used———————————————————————————

Bequest and receipt clause for a bequest to a charity
I GIVE the sum of (*insert the amount in words and figures*) to (*insert the correct name of the charity and its registered number*) if it shall still operate for charitable purposes when I die. This legacy shall be used for its general charitable purposes and I declare that the receipt of the person who seems to my trustees to be the treasurer or other proper officer of the charity shall be a sufficient discharge to my trustees for the bequest and that my trustees shall not be obliged to see how the bequest is used———————————————————————

In a will which contains a gift for life or time-contingent interest

Power of investment
MY TRUSTEES shall have power to invest the assets of my estate and vary investments in all respects as if they were their own and to borrow upon the security of the assets and investments upon such terms and for such purposes as they think fit———————————————————

Exclusion of the rules of apportionment
I DECLARE that there shall be no apportionment of the income of my estate to the intent that the Apportionment Act 1870 and the equitable rules of apportionment shall be excluded from the administration of my estate———————————————————————————

Advancement clause
MY TRUSTEES shall have power in their sole discretion to use part or the entirety of the income and capital of my estate to which a beneficiary may become entitled for the benefit of the beneficiary

Personal benefit by trustees
MY TRUSTEES may exercise or refrain from exercising the powers contained in my will notwithstanding that in doing so any of them shall benefit personally provided that they act in good faith_____

Exclusion of statutory provisions relating to trustees' duty to consult with beneficiaries and beneficiaries' power to appoint and remove trustees
THE FOLLOWING statutory provisions shall not apply to my will or to any codicil hereto: sections 11 (1) and 19 of the Trusts of Land and Appointment of Trustees Act 1996_____

In the will of a testator involved in a business

IF I am involved in any business at the date of my death either as a sole proprietor or partner my executors shall have full power to continue to carry it on either alone or in a partnership or through an agent or agents for the benefit of my estate and they shall be entitled to be indemnified out of my estate against any debts or liabilities reasonably incurred in carrying on the business_____

SPECIMEN FORM OF CODICIL

BY THIS (*insert first, second or as appropriate*) CODICIL

to my last will dated (*insert the date of the will*) I (*insert your full names address and occupation, if any*)_____

1.___(*insert clauses to carry out the changes which you wish to make to the will*)_____

2.___IN all other respects I CONFIRM my said will_____

IN WITNESS whereof I have signed this codicil this   day of   Two thousand and   _____

SIGNED by the said (*insert your full names*)
as a (*insert 'first' or 'second' as appropriate*)
codicil to (*insert 'his' or 'her' as appropriate*)   } Testator to sign
last will in our joint presence and then by   here
us in (*insert 'his' or 'her' as appropriate*)

First witness to sign here

and print his name here

and write his address and occupation, if any, here

Second witness to sign here

and print his name here

and write his address and occupation, if any, here

SPECIMEN ATTESTATION CLAUSES FOR USE IN WILLS AND CODICILS IN SPECIAL SITUATIONS

Attestation clause for use in the will or codicil of a testator who cannot write but makes his mark

SIGNED by the said (*insert full names of*   Testator
the testator) by making his mark in our joint   to make
presence after the document had been read   } his mark
over to him and he appeared to approve it   here
and understand it perfectly and then signed
by us in his presence

First witness to sign here

and print his name here

and write his address and occupation, if any, here

Second witness to sign here

and print his name here

and write his address and occupation, if any, here

Note: Instead of the clause in the skeleton will which begins 'I N W I T-N E S S' insert the following clause:

I N W I T N E S S whereof I have set my hand to this my (*insert will or codicil as appropriate*) this   day of   Two thousand and   _____

Attestation clause for use in the will or codicil of a testator who cannot make a mark or write

SIGNED by (*insert full names and address of the person signing*) at the request and on behalf of the said (*insert the full names of the testator*) to give effect to this his (*insert will or codicil as appropriate*) after the said (*insert 'will' or 'codicil' here*) had been read over to him and he seemed to understand it perfectly and approve it, the signing and reading over having taken place in the presence of the said (*insert the full names of the testator*) and in the joint presence of the following witnesses who then signed in the joint presence of the said (*insert the full names of the testator*) and the said (*insert the full names of the person who signed on behalf of the testator*) and each other.

(*The person signing to sign his name here*) on behalf of (*and insert the testator's name here*)

First witness to sign here

and print his name here.

and write his address and occupation, if any, here.

Second witness to sign here

and print his name here

and write his address and occupation, if any, here.

Note. Instead of the clause in the skeleton will which begins 'I N W I T N E S S' insert the following clause:

'I N W I T N E S S whereof I have caused this my (*insert will or codicil as appropriate*) to be signed this   day of   Two thousand and   _____'

Attestation clause for use in the will or codicil of a testator who is blind

SIGNED on behalf of the said (*insert the full names of the testator*) (who is blind) at his request to give effect to this his (*insert will or codicil as appropriate*) by (*insert full names and address of the person signing*) after the (*insert will or codicil as appropriate*) had been read over to (*insert the full names of the testator*) and he seemed to understand and approve the (*insert 'will' or 'codicil' as appropriate*) perfectly the signing and reading over having taken place in the joint presence of the said (*insert the full names of the testator*) and the following witnesses who then signed in the presence of the said (*insert full names of the person signing*) and of (*insert the full names of the testator*) and each other.

(*The person signing to sign his name here*) on behalf of (*and insert the testator's full names here*).

First witness to sign here

and print his name here

and write his address and occupation, if any, here.

Second witness to sign here

and print his name here

and write his address and occupation, if any, here.

Note. Instead of the clause in the skeleton will which begins 'I N W I T N E S S' insert the following clause:

IN WITNESS whereof I have caused this my (*insert will or codicil as appropriate*) to be signed on my behalf this   day of   Two thousand and   _____

SPECIMEN FORM OF ADVANCE DECISION OR LIVING WILL

1. I (*insert your full names, address and occupation, if any*), on the (*insert the date*) make this Advance Decision and set down as guidance to my family and my medical practitioners these directions as to the types of medical treatment I wish and do not wish to undergo if in the future I suffer from any of the conditions set out in the First Schedule below and I am unable to think rationally and/or to express my wishes.

2. IN giving these directions I consider that

- ◆ I am in good physical health
- ◆ I am mentally competent
- ◆ I have considered the matter thoroughly
- ◆ I believe myself to be fully informed and to perfectly understand the information relevant to the decision I make and
- ◆ I give these directions voluntarily and free from pressure or influence by others.

3. IF any of the conditions specified in the First Schedule below apply to me and in the opinion of (*insert number*) medical practitioners I am unlikely to recover a good quality of life THEN I wish attempts to be made to prolong my life by the treatments specified in the Second Schedule below if they are appropriate but do not wish to undergo any of the treatments specified in the Third Schedule below, even though the withholding of such treatments puts my life at risk.

The First Schedule referred to above – the conditions.

- ◆ I am brain dead.
- ◆ I show no signs of cerebral activity.
- ◆ I am suffering from permanent mental impairment and incapable of thinking rationally.
- ◆ I have been in a continuous coma for (*insert the number*) months.
- ◆ By reason of an impairment or disturbance in the functioning of my brain or my mind I have been unable to recognise and respond to my family or friends and I have not been aware of my surroundings or able to differentiate between night and day for (*insert the number*) of months.
- ◆ I am so disabled that I am completely dependent upon others and my condition is unlikely to improve.

- I am suffering from any degenerative and incurable illness.
- I have suffered (*insert the number*) cardiac arrests.
- I am totally paralysed.
- I am blind, dumb and deaf.
- I am in a persistent vegetative state.

<u>The Second Schedule</u> referred to above – treatment I wish to have if appropriate even though I am unlikely to recover a good quality of life and such treatment might put my life at risk.

- Artificial feeding.
- Attempted resuscitation.
- Drug therapy.
- Blood transfusions.
- Artificial ventilation.
- Treatment to alleviate pain.
- Treatment in respect of which the risks are high compared with its likely benefits.

<u>The Third Schedule</u> referred to above – treatment I do not wish to have even though the withholding of such treatment might put my life at risk.

- Attempted resuscitation.
- Artificial feeding.
- Drug therapy.
- Blood transfusions.
- Artificial ventilation.
- Treatment in respect of which the risks are high compared with its likely benefits.

<u>SIGNED</u> by me (*insert your full names*)
in the presence of (*insert full names of*   *Sign your name here*
the witness)

*Witness to sign here and to print full
names and address here*

Note. The conditions and treatments set out in the schedules are specimens only and you will need to amend and omit or add to them to suit your own wishes but any attempt to prevent basic care such as feeding by mouth or washing will be ineffective.

Checklist
For Use After You Have Prepared
Your Will But Before You Sign It

Have you included or considered the following matters which have been discussed in the preceding text?:

The date the will is made.

Your full names (including any alias or nicknames in which you have property) and your status or occupation and address.

The executor's full names and status or occupation and address.

Have you included a co-executor or an alternative executor and his full names and status or occupation and address in case your first choice dies before you?

Are you contemplating marriage to a particular person in the near future or entering into a registered civil partnership?

Have you set out in your will or in an accompanying letter any burial/cremation/funeral wishes about which you feel strongly?

Have you checked whether any property you own with another person is owned as beneficial joint tenants or tenants in common and remembered that any land or property of which you are a beneficial joint tenant cannot be left in your will and will pass to your co-owner on your death unless you sever the joint tenancy? If there is any jointly owned property in respect of which you are a beneficial joint tenant and which you wish to leave by your will, you should sever the beneficial joint tenancy and create a tenancy in common in your lifetime. You cannot sever it by your will.

Are any pecuniary legacies you have left to bear their share of inheritance tax or is the tax on them to be paid out of the residuary estate?

Are any gifts of specific articles you are leaving to bear their share of inheritance tax or is the tax on them to be paid out of the residuary estate?

What is to happen to the residue of your estate, or the share of the residuary estate as the case might be, if the named beneficiary dies before you?

Do you wish to make any of your bequests contingent upon the happening of any event, for example contingent upon survival by a specified period or the attainment of a specified age?

Do you wish your executors to have power, in their discretion, to use money from a bequest or from the income it produces for the benefit of beneficiaries whose gift is contingent upon the happening of any event (for example contingent upon survival by a specified period or the attainment of a specified age) before the event has occurred?

Have you stated who is to be entitled to give your executors a valid receipt and discharge for any gift to a charity or to an under age beneficiary?

If you are a father and were not married to any of your children's mothers at the time of the child's birth, has a parental responsibility agreement been completed and registered or does one need to be registered or completed?

If you are a father and were not married to any of your children's mothers at the time of the child's birth, do you need to have the child's birth re-registered to show you as the father in the registration particulars?

Have you appointed a guardian for any infant children you might leave and in respect of whom you have parental responsibility? Have you made provision in your will for their maintenance from the estate?

In the absence of fraud or gross negligence on their part, are your trustees to be relieved from responsibility for any mistakes they might make?

Do you wish to exclude any excludable statutory provisions?

Do you wish your executors to have additional powers to those always given to them by law, for example power to purchase assets from your estate, or to increase their powers to continue any business you have or to advance monies to contingent beneficiaries or the executors' powers of investment?

Do you wish your executors to receive a legacy or payment for the work they do on behalf of the estate? If so, unless they are professional trustees, you must include a clause in the will expressly authorising payment.

Do you wish to include a clause to the effect that legatees shall receive interest on their legacies calculated from the date of your death instead of the usual rule that they are only entitled to interest calculated from the date of death if the legacies are not paid to them within one year of death? Such interest is, of course, paid out of your residuary estate and at the expense of those to whom you have left your residuary estate.

Have you considered any unusual family circumstances you may have, such as a disabled spouse or children and any beneficiaries with special needs?

Have you made sufficient provision in your will to prevent challenges being made to it under the Inheritance (Provision for Family and Dependants) Act 1975 as amended and do you wish to leave a statement indicating why you have made no provision or only limited provision for possible claimants?

Have you considered the effect of any previous marriages, civil partnerships and divorce settlements and whether they exclude any claim against your estate? If they do not, consider whether or not you have made reasonable provision for possible claimants e.g. an ex-spouse who has not remarried, by your will.

Have you made it clear whether any legacies are to be paid in addition to or in substitution for any debts you owe to your beneficiaries?

Have you made a will to deal with any property you own which is not in England or Wales and is that will in accordance with the law of the relevant state in which the property is situated, both as to the formalities for making the will and the substantive law of that country?

Do you need to say in your will in what state you consider yourself to be domiciled?

Is it appropriate to state in the will whether it is a mirror will or mutual will?

Have the trustees of any pension scheme of which you are a member been notified of the way in which you wish them to exercise any discretion they may have in relation to any potential benefits arising from your membership?

Have you considered the effect of inheritance tax on your estate? Could your will be made more tax efficient and still carry out your wishes? Have you considered making nil rate band gifts, the needs of your surviving spouse and the assets and income which she has in her own right, whether or not a survivorship clause should be included in the will, what are the needs of the individual beneficiaries and whether a generation should be skipped?

Have you included in your will everyone you wish to benefit?

Have you considered what is to happen to any pets you might own at your death and included the appropriate provisions in your will?

FOR USE AFTER YOU HAVE SIGNED AND COMPLETED YOUR WILL

Place the will in a safe place.

Have you informed your executors and your family where the will can be found and if appropriate, supplied them with a copy that is clearly marked 'copy'?

Have you created a file of the information your executors will require (as explained in Chapter 11), placed it with the will or in some other safe place and notified your executors of its existence and where it can be found?

Glossary

Absolutely – not for the benefit of any other person and free from any condition.

Administrator – the person who winds up the matters left behind after death by a person who does not make a will or who does not appoint anyone who is able and willing to wind them up.

Advance Decision – see Living Will.

Affidavit – a document the contents of which have been sworn on oath to be true.

Affirm – the word used to mean the making of a solemn declaration by a person who for reasons of conscience declines to swear on oath.

Annulment – making void.

Articles of association – a document which governs how a company is structured and managed including the various classes of the company's share capital and the rights of each class of shares.

Beneficiary – an organisation or person who benefits from or inherits.

Bequest – an article or sum of money left to a person or organisation by a will or codicil.

Capital Gains Tax – the tax which is levied upon the increase in value of an asset at the time it is disposed of.

Chattels – moveable property.

Civil partner – a person who entered into the relationship with another person of the same sex which is recognised by the Civil Partnership Act 2004 and registered that relationship in accordance with the terms of the Act.

Co-executor – an executor who is appointed to act with another executor.

Co-habitees – unmarried people who live together as man and wife.

Codicil – a supplementary document which adds to or amends an existing will.

Contingent – dependent upon the fulfilment of a condition or the happening of an event.

Deceased – dead, the person who has died.

Discretionary Trust – a trust under which no specific person has a present entitlement to the trust funds and under which the funds are allocated amongst named potential beneficiaries in the discretion of the trustees.

Domicile – the state or country in which you intend to make your permanent home. For a fuller explanation of the meaning of domicile see Chapter 3.

Donee – a person to whom something is given.

Donor – a person who makes a gift.

Estate – the assets and property which are owned at death.

Executor/executrix – the person or company appointed by a will or codicil to carry out its provisions after the death of the person who makes it.

Gifts per capita – gifts by which each person named or in the defined group of beneficiaries, (e.g. 'my children') takes an equal share. Contrast this with gifts described as being given per stirpes. If a gift is given to a group 'per stirpes' those who inherit through their parent take equally between them their parent's share and not an equal share with their parent or with the other members of their parent's class. If a gift is described as being given per stirpes (as opposed to being given per capita) it means that descendants do not compete for a share of the gift with an immediate ancestor who is still alive.

Gifts per stirpes – *see* gifts per capita.

Grant of representation – the document given out by the Probate Registry which gives legal authority to deal with matters relating to someone who has died. The document is a grant of probate if the deceased made a valid will appointing an executor who proves the will or a grant of letters of administration if he did not.

Guardian – a person given the powers and responsibilities of a parent in respect of an underage child.

Inheritance tax – the tax charged on gifts, usually, but not exclusively, gifts made by a person on his death.

Intestate – not having made a valid will or someone who dies without a valid will.

Intestacy – the absence of a valid will.

Joint tenants – people who jointly own assets in such a way that by law the ownership passes to the survivor or survivors on the death of one of them.

Legacy – a gift or money left by a will or by a codicil.

Legatee – a beneficiary to whom a gift is made by a will or a codicil.

Letters of administration – the document issued by the Probate Registry which confirms the right of an administrator (the person appointed by the Probate Registry) to administer the estate of a person who has not made a valid will or who has made a valid will of which there is no executor who is willing and able to act.

Life interest – the right to benefit from something during life but not to dispose of it on death.

Life tenant – a person who has the right to benefit from something during life but not to dispose of it on death.

Living Will – a statement which sets out what medical treatment the person concerned wishes to have or does not wish to have in specified circumstances.

Minor – a person who is under the age of 18 and who has consequently not reached the age of majority.

Next of kin – the nearest relative as defined by the intestacy law.

Nil-rate band – the part of an estate the value of which is below the value at which inheritance tax is charged.

Personal representatives – those given authority to represent someone who has died and to administer that person's affairs – executors or administrators if no executors prove a will.

PETs (Potentially Exempt Transfers) – gifts that are exempt from inheritance tax at the time they are made but which become liable to the tax if the donor does not survive the making of the gift by seven years.

Power of appointment – the right to decide who shall have the benefit of an asset or benefit from the income it produces.

Predecease – die before.

Probate – the document issued by the Probate Registry after a death which proves that the deceased's will is valid and authorises the executor to deal with the estate.

Probate Registry – the office of the High Court which deals with matters relating to estates after death.

Residue or residuary estate – that part of an estate which is left after all funeral and legal expenses, inheritance tax, debts, liabilities and legacies have been discharged.

Revoke – cancel.

Revocation – cancellation.

Spouse – the person to whom you are married.

Tenant in common – someone who owns a share of an asset in such a way the he can deal with it separately from the remainder of the asset.

Testator – a male person who makes a will.

Testatrix – a female person who makes a will.

Trustee – a person who is trusted to carry out or perform a duty or service or hold or manage property for the benefit of another person.

Useful Addresses

Law stationers

Oyez Straker (see website for local retail shops). Tel: 0845 217 7565.
  Website: *www.oyezformslink.co.uk*

Shaw & Sons, Shaway House, 21 Bourne Park Road, Crayford,
  Kent DA1 4BZ. Tel: 01322 621109 for customer services; 0800
  018 1750 for orders. Website: *www.shaws.co.uk*

Stat Plus, London Head Office, Unit 4, 500 Purley Way, Croydon,
  Surrey CRO 4NZ. Tel: 020 8774 3453. Fax: 020 8760 0510.
  Website: *www.statplus.co.uk* Other branches in Birmingham,
  Leeds, Bristol, Manchester and Edinburgh.

Charities

The Blue Cross, Freepost OF224, Room L335, Shilton Road,
  Burford, Oxon OX18 4PF. Tel: 01993 823083.
  Website: *www.bluecross.org.uk*

The Charity Commission, P O Box 1227, Liverpool L69 3UG.
  Tel: 0845 3000 218. Website *www.charity-commission.gov.uk*

The Dogs Trust, 17 Wakeley Street, London EC1V 7RQ.
  Tel: 020 7837 0006 betweeen 9.00 a.m and 5.00 p.m. on
  Mondays to Fridays. Website: *www.dogstrust.org.uk*

The RSPCA, Freepost SEA1050 03, Horsham RH13 9RS.
  Tel: 0300 123 4555. Website: *www.homeforlife.org.uk* or
  www.rspca.org.uk

Miscellaneous

The Natural Death Centre, In The Hill House, Watley Lane,
  Twyford, Winchester, SO21 1QX. Tel: 0871 228 2098.

Fax: 020 7354 3831. Website: *www.naturaldeath.org.uk*

The NHS Organ Donor Register, UK Transplant, Fox Den Road, Stoke Gifford, Bristol BS34 8RR. Tel: 0300 123 2323. Fax: 0117 975 7577. Website: *www.uktransplant.org.uk*

Office of the Public Guardian, PO Box 15118, Birmingham, B16 6GX. Tel: 0845 330 2900. Fax: 020 7664 7551. Email: *customerservices@publicguardian.gsi.gov.uk*. Website: *www.publicguardian.gov.uk*

The Principal Probate Registry, 1st Avenue House, 42–49 High Holborn, London WC1V 6NP. Tel: 020 7947 7000.

Index

Tell A he'll want several copies of my Death Certificate — clearing up cash accounts & investments will require a copy for each to see. Usually they return these fairly quickly. for their charitable purposes.

funeral arrangements

Capital Gains/Inheritance Tax.

Tax

If either or both of my nieces dies before me their share of my estate is to be ~~If my estate is to be~~ divided between 7,000 & equally

Miriam to get

Alice 7,000

	1	1/10
	2	1/10
	3	1/10
		7/10 to be divided the equally between children of the above, alive at the day of my death, namely —

n. o
~~CDTE~~

= =

Executor. ___ If my nephew A. B. die. before me Miriam to get his ___ If either of my nieces dies before me, then their share is to